# A TIME FOR FUSION

## A Spiritual Guide for America to Work Toward Globalization and a Coalition of Nations

William H. Calhoun, Ph. D.

authorHOUSE®

*AuthorHouse™ LLC*
*1663 Liberty Drive*
*Bloomington, IN 47403*
*www.authorhouse.com*
*Phone: 1-800-839-8640*

*Published by AuthorHouse    05/14/2014*

*ISBN: 978-1-4918-6714-3 (sc)*
*ISBN: 978-1-4918-6715-0 (e)*

*Library of Congress Control Number: 2014903619*

# CONTENTS

## Part I

# Part II: Opening The Door To Fusion

# Part III: East And West In Fusion

## **Part IV**: Toward A New World Order

**The Mandala on the cover is from:**
**The Wikipedia file titled Mandala**

(Source: Own Work By R. Gopakumar http://en.wikipedia.org/wiki/
File:T he_Birth_of_the_son_of_God.jpg)

A Mandala is a spiritual and ritual symbol used in Hinduism and Buddhism representing the universe. Carl Jung first introduced the mandala to the west and used it with some of his patients. He found patients who constructed a mandala were able to focus their energy on this task much as they might do during meditation. Mandalas have a healing effect when used in art therapy. Jung thought his patients created a sacred space uniquely theirs. The mandala served to bring together what seemed to be irreconcilable opposites and to bridge across the space between hopeless conflict. Thus for us the mandala is a symbol for fusion of east and west.

William H. Calhoun.

# ACKNOWLEDGEMENTS

Many persons have contributed to my thinking about the topic I call Fusion. I was introduced to some of the concepts of Buddhism by ministers and friends in the Tennessee Valley and Westside Unitarian Universalist Churches in Knoxville, Tennessee. Once interested, I began to read further with books such as those by Thich Nhat Hanh who is a prolific writer and I am most indebted to him for the book *Living Buddha, Living Christ*. That book showed that the religion and philosophies of the East and West can meld. I also acknowledge the writings of the Dalai Lamas of which *The Universe in a Single Atom* is the most ecumenical book I have encountered.

I thank Jerry Morton for introducing me to *A Course in Miracles*. That book became a major force in my life, and I used a great deal of the material in my earlier book *From Warrior to Sage*. *The Course* is a major bridge between the *Hebrew Bible*, the *Christian Bible*, and *Attitudinal Healing*.

I thank all the people at Oasis Institute in Knoxville which is our local center for Attitudinal Healing. I especially appreciate the time and patience shown by the Executive Director, Stephen Anthony. From these sources I began to see the juncture of Eastern religion, as typified by Buddhism, and Western religion, as typified as the Judaic-Christian tradition which is interpreted in *A Course in Miracles* and the further interpretation of *The Course* by Gerald Jampolsky (*Teach Only Love*) who developed his system of Attitudinal Healing which has become a world-wide program for healing.

More recently my youngest son directed me to the new book by Jeffery Sachs, *The Price of Civilization,* in which he brought into our economic thinking the concept of mindfulness as it is used in Buddhism. For me things seemed to fall into place. For example, Sachs viewed Aristotle as the spokesperson for Western thinking and Buddha for Eastern thinking and I share that perspective. But, more to the point, Sachs was writing about America in its current state and how mindfulness, and the Buddhist's idea of the middle path, could help set America on the course for citizen involvement in decision making and to return a sense of civility to the media which surrounds us everywhere.

I especially wish to thank Merry Levering, who is a professor of religious studies with Buddhism as her major area of interest. At this time she is living in Tokyo, Japan and teaching Buddhism, although she was born in America and taught at the University of Tennessee for many years, and was active in the Westside U. U. Church in Farragut, TN.

These diverse events placed within the context of modern American society need to be acknowledged. We Americans are suffering from a serious polarization of major political, economic, and religious leaders, which leaves no option for the middle way. The *Middle Way* is the path of the Buddha. The idea of mindfulness is captured when the Buddha replied to questions about what he was, with the simple statement: "I am awake."

I thank my Tuesday Luncheon group for tolerating me and my book. Thank you all.


William (Bill) H. Calhoun Knoxville, Tennessee

# FUSION

*The act or process of fusing or the state of being fused.*

***OR***

*The body resulting from such a coalition.*

*Combining widely differing ethnic and regional*

*. . . religions and philosophies.*

**From: The Online Dictionary**

# PREFACE

F usion offers a summary review of my life which may be my final comments on contemporary society, religion, philosophy, and the world order. This is quite a task and I am humble as I offer my insights for your consideration. I recently turned eighty with the clear recognition that I am at the autumn of my life, but I have a story I want to tell of my experiences during those years. In writing Fusion I attempt to make sense of this world with its stresses, challenges, anxieties, and dangers facing our next generations. I also recognize the beauty of the natural world, the pleasure in watching my grand-children mature, seeing the outcome of some of my personal projects, and the sheer amazement when I stare at a starry sky, watch a bird build a nest, and see the birth of young. There is so much beauty in this world. May all of you find that beauty?

I began life in California in 1932 as the son of a farmer and a boy of the soil. I have lost that link to the earth although I have a garden and do raise some home-grown tomatoes. World War II had ended and America was on a high and I was attracted to the freedom and joy of flight. After two years of college I followed my bliss by entering naval aviation training at Pensacola, FL in July of 1952 as a member of class 32-52 of Naval Aviation Cadets. I completed flight training in 1954 including transition to jet aircraft and joined the squadron VC-3 at Moffett Field near Mountain View, CA, as a junior aviator. I later transferred to a newly formed squadron, VF-194, a part of Carrier Air Group Nine and embarked on a 5 month cruise aboard the U. S. S. Oriskany (CVA-34) in February of 1956. I was a reserve officer with a four-year commitment and when my time was up, I chose not to continue on active duty. I was now married to Lois Ann Heikens and we planned to have a family. I applied to and was accepted at Stanford University although like many re-entry students did not know what I wanted to do with my life but I gravitated toward psychology in which I earned the B. A. degree in 1959. By this time I had the confidence and grades to apply for graduate school at U. C. Berkeley and was admitted with financial support. I studied biological psychology and received the PhD. in 1964. I applied for and was offered a position at the University of Tennessee in Knoxville which I accepted.

No one's life ends with commencement as graduation is only a starting point in one's life-long journey. I enjoyed teaching and doing laboratory research; I earned tenure and promotion and served as the Head of the Department from 1975 to 1986. Soon after coming to Tennessee my wife and I became active in the Unitarian church in Knoxville and I began a spiritual journey that is ongoing. During this time I did have a year away on a post-doc at Indiana University where I did hands on research with rats and published several papers. I also met John Young who was a new minister to the Unitarian Church in Bloomington, IN. He had studied eastern religions and opened me to a journey of the study of life, spirituality, religion, and Buddhism.

When I left the Headship I found time to start a serious in depth study of psychology and spirituality. As my teaching methods evolved, I found that if I listened to my students, I could learn much from them. At this time I adopted a strategy akin to how one mentors students. I used popular books relevant to daily life and asked the students to write from the heart. They did so. I extended my interests and was motivated to attend a year-long Workshop with Carol Pearson who was an advocate of Archetypal Psychology and had used archetypes to classify developmental stages of life (*The Hero*

*Within*, 1986; *Awakening the Heroes Within*, 1991). I have written about this experience in *From Warrior to Sage* (Calhoun, 2006).

I was introduced to *A Course in Miracles* which was a great eye-opener. I became involved with an Attitudinal Healing group using the materials developed by Gerald Jamplosky based on *A Course in Miracles*. More recently I began to see the complementary nature of Buddhism and Attitudinal Healing and sought out specific examples of the joining of these two approaches to life.

Recently my son Brad introduced me to Jeffery Sachs (*The Price of Civilization*, 2011) who brought the notion of mindfulness, a cornerstone of Buddhism, into application in American economic practice. I saw this as a great way to express my sense that it is time for the East and West to recognize the complimentary aspects of their philosophy and religion and bring together the best parts of both in what I call fusion. I will outline the benefits from this endeavor for myself and how it may work for others.

As the Greek teacher Dr. Papaderos in Robert Fulghum's book *It Was On Fire When I Lay Down On It (1989)* answered Fulghum's question about the meaning of life, I will answer the same question. Papaderos replied to Fulghum by stating that:

"I am a fragment of a mirror whose whole design and shape I do not know. Nevertheless, with what I have I can reflect light into the dark places of this world—into the black places in the hearts of men—and change some things in some people. Perhaps others may see and do likewise." (P. 177). He concluded by saying this was what he was about. "This is the meaning of my life."

I have a small mirror which one of my students gave to me when I spoke about this story in my class. I hope to reflect some light into a few dark places, and perhaps someone will watch and do likewise.

# Introduction

# THE TWAIN SHALL MEET

*"Oh, East is east, and West is West, and never the twain shall meet,*
*Till Earth and Sky stand presently at God's great Judgment Seat;*
*But there is neither East nor West, Border, nor breed, nor Birth,*
*When two strong men stand face to face.*
*tho' they come from the ends of the earth"!*

*Rudyard Kipling, 1889*

Rudyard Kipling was writing about the life in India when the British occupied the country and contrasted thoughts and actions of the native (the East) and the British (the West). Much of what he wrote was true for that time and continued up to the time that the British left India in 1947. If we evaluate Kipling's comments today, we find things are very different, and it is a time for the twain to meet. During the time that Britain's empire circled the globe, it had a large navy and could control large areas of the world with its navy and the use of colonial forces. That empire ended during World War II and things have never been the same. Travel to the east today is relatively short in comparison to what it was in 1900, and many people have traveled to the east and many have traveled to the west. A significant number of Americans have gone to the east to encounter the religions and philosophies of the east to work on their personal journey. A group of Americans who did go to the east returned to found a college for the advanced study of eastern religion, Naropa University, in Colorado. The strict dividing line between east and west of Kipling's day is no longer true and we find a beginning of fusion of east and west in these undertakings.

My goal in this work is to show that eastern and western philosophy and religion have a great deal in common and the divide is artificial and need not be continued. As a preface to this material I need to explain my bias. I think of myself as a person who tries to clump together things rather than separate them into smaller and smaller parts. A wise person once said that people fall into two general categories; these categories are clumpers and splitters. Those who clump things together seek to find common areas which can pull or clump together groups of things. Splitters on the other hand strive to highlight differences among things and split or separate them into smaller and smaller groups. It should be clear that my intent is to clump together eastern and western thought in contrast to what Kipling sought to do.

A prime example of an effort to clump east and west is found in the recent book by Thich Nhat Hanh titled *Living Buddha, Living Christ.* Let us use these two persons as symbols for the two strong men who do stand face-to-face and share their essence. Thick Nhat Hanh is a Buddhist monk and has written many books, several of which try to make Buddhism clear to westerners, and to demonstrate the commonalities of the Christian and Buddhist beliefs and practices. For this reason, I will use *Living Buddha, Living Christ* for much of this section of my book. By some standards, Buddhism is not a religion as there is no God as in the Christian religion and the idea of salvation is foreign to Buddhist practitioners.

Yet, let me refer to Thich Nhat Hanh as he wrote:

> "A year ago in Florence, a Catholic priest told me
> that he was interested in learning more about Buddhism. I
> asked him to share with me his understanding of the "Holy
> Spirit" and he replied,
>
> 'The Holy Spirit is the energy sent by God.' His
> statement made me glad. It confirmed my feeling that the
> safest way to approach the Trinity is through the door of
> the Holy Spirit." (Pp13-14.)

From this quote, I will refute the argument that Buddhism lacks a God as they refer to the Holy Spirit in much the same way Christians refer to God. The major difference is that Christians often think of God as having human characteristics. The Holy Spirit is a concept rather than a person. A second point is that Christians often appeal to God for help whereas the easterner sees the Holy Spirit as a source for the individual to find his or her own way.

Regarding how persons see their role in the world, there is an interesting story about a group of builders constructing a church in France. One of the local Priests visited the structure and one-by-one approached each group of builders and asked them what they were doing. The stone masons lifted pieces of stone they had worked on and pointed to the walls they were building. The carpenters demonstrated sawing and cutting and how to assemble a section of the roof. The plumbers bragged about the cistern and how it would bring holy water into the church.

As the day was ending the workers began to leave but an old woman stayed to sweep up the excess materials to clear the way for the workers the next day. When the priest asked her what she was doing, she immediately replied: "I'm building a church." The sweeper was well aware of what she was doing and how it fitted into the totality of the church. When the Buddhist says I am sitting, he is aware of the moment as he sits. This old woman, as she swept up the leavings, knew she was building a church.

# My Country

### by
### An Antebellum II Man

*We were taught the history of our country*
*We learned that Columbus discovered America*

*George Washington was the father of our country*
*Abraham Lincoln gave an address at Gettysburg*

*We sang God Bless America in our classes*
*We raised the American flag each morning*

*We were taught that we had never lost a war*
*Our soldiers came home to an Armistice Day*
*parade*

*We found out that politicians lied to us*
*We didn't win in Korea; we lost in Vietnam*
*We have hate groups that want America to be*
*a white, European nation*

*We outspend the rest of the world with war*
*Machines*
*But we are not at peace at home or abroad*

*We are seen as a bully by other nations*
*Yet, I still place my hand over my heart*
*when singing the National Anthem*

# PART I

Source: Le penseur de la Porte de l'Enfer (musée Rodin)

# INTRODUCTION

# WHERE ARE WE TODAY?

I t is a propitious time in the history of America. We have only recently emerged from the most serious economic and political downturn since the great depression of 1929. It is time for us as a nation to take a moment to rethink our past and see if we can plan for a new path into the future. Jeffery D. Sachs is a world known economist who wrote a serious dissection of the policies of the administrators of the U. S. Government beginning with Ronald Reagan's program of reducing taxes and eliminating regulations. Sachs wrote: "When the U. S. economy hit the skids in the 1970s, the political Right, represented by Ronald Reagan, claimed that government was to blame for its growing ills." (Sachs, *The Price of Civilization*, 2011, p. 7). Sachs wrote that "This diagnosis, although incorrect, had a plausible ring to it to enough Americans to enable the Reagan coalition to begin a process of dismantling effective government programs and undermining the government's capacity to help steer the economy." The continuation of this policy through George W. Bush eventually led to the serious economic problems of the 21st century that nearly brought America to its knees.

Sachs used the theme of being mindful as a message to the American people as a major part of reawakening American virtue and prosperity. Sachs in Chapter 9 wrote of *The Mindful Society*. He outlined steps to be taken to develop a new American economy, a healthier society and a more ethical basis for the study and practice of economics itself. Sachs argued that the rich in America have abandoned their commitment of social responsibility and instead have adopted the theme of chasing personal wealth and personal power, ". . . the rest of society be damned."

The mindful society, according to Sachs, will aid us as citizens of America to avoid the many distractions of consumerism in the media and to look inward for that personal soul as a guide to ethical living.

## The Mindful Society

"'The unexamined life is not worth living.' said Socrates. We might equally say that the unexamined economy is not capable of securing our well-being. Our greatest national illusion is that a healthy society can be organized around the single-minded pursuit of wealth". (P. 9) "Two of humanity's greatest sages, Buddha in the Eastern tradition and Aristotle in the Western tradition, counseled us wisely about humanity's innate tendency to chase transient illusions rather than to keep our minds and lives focused on deeper, longer-term sources of well-being. Both urged us to keep to a middle path, to cultivate moderation and virtue in our personal behavior and attitudes despite the allures of extremes. Both urged us to look after our personal needs without forgetting our compassion toward others in society. Both cautioned that the single-minded pursuit of wealth and consumption leads to addictions and compulsions rather than to happiness and the virtues of a life well lived. Throughout the ages, other great sages, from Confucius to Adam Smith to Mahatma Gandhi and the Dalai Lama, have joined the call for moderation and compassion as the pillars of a good society." (P. 9.)

Some of the signs of these issues include the economic crisis in Europe and America which seems to be at the head of the list. The United States and Europe suffered a serious economic decline with the associated fears of job loss and bank failures to plague the masses. We are only beginning to come to grips with the notion that the entire world is inter-connected and that we cannot go it alone as the neoconservative movement led by George W. Bush thought when we brought war to Iraq and Afghanistan. We should have paid more attention to the failures in Korea and Vietnam when making the decisions to take war to the middle-east. Imagine what we would have thought if Truman in 1956 had told us that there would be U. S. military forces in Korea fifty plus years after the truce and that we would continue to pay for troops to be stationed in Europe into the 21st century. But that is what has happened with huge costs in trying to maintain a sense of military dominance of the world by the U. S.

This is not just an American fear but a global fear with Europe in turmoil, Russia now playing a secondary role in world affairs, and Asia emerging as the next global empire. This fear is most strong in the bottom half of the citizens who struggle to make it with low paying jobs and only begrudging, modest government help. The unions have only helped to bring on the problems in the American auto industry, and the take-home pay of the upper echelon is staggeringly out of proportion to their worth to the country. How did we get to this place in time?

There are several significant issues which are part of this problem and we will work through them in order.

- We are caught up in an argumentative milieu.
- The demise of the unifying concept of Western Civilization.

5

- The Geo-political re-organization of the European sphere of influence.
- The fallacy that we are Number ONE. We are a great nation, but not the greatest nation.
- In spite of our huge military machine, we cannot rule the world.
- Our economic philosophy is in serious disorder for many reasons.

# CHAPTER ONE

# WHY ARE AMERICANS SO HARSH AND POLARIZED

## What happened to fairness in America?

Once:

- Drug companies did not advertise.
- Lawyers had a low profile.
- New programs were balanced.
- Radio and TV reported the news.

A well-known linguist wrote about The Argument Culture which seems rampant in America today. She wrote: "The argument culture urges us to approach the world and the people in it from an adversarial frame of mind." On television people argue rather than discuss, and take extreme positions without any regard to a middle ground. We set up debates in which the two participants take opposing sides in which they express the most extreme, polarized views as if there were only two sides to all issues. In the argument culture we find common military metaphors as the war against poverty, the battle against cancer, the war against drugs, fighting for their life, winning the latest war against cancer, the fight against Alzheimer's, the battle of the sexes proliferate. Tannen offers the suggestion that we move beyond debate into dialogue. For example, talk less about rights, and more about needs, and do not speak harshly about those who disagree with your personal beliefs.

Persons born in the first half of the 20th century will probably have noticed a major shift in how the media present news and advertisers present information. Once we had agreements not to publicly seek legal cases and drug companies relied on drugstores to advertise their wares. The American Bar Association had restrictions on what an attorney could put in the yellow pages. Slowly those strictures against advertising have evaporated and we are bombarded with commercials about new drugs and how we can get a settlement in court for some damage. The media presented a balanced view on news and most people felt they could trust the media to present information that was based on fact. In 1949 the Federal Communications Commission (FCC) adopted a proposition called "The Fairness Doctrine." This doctrine was to apply to any organization holding a license regulated by the FCC to offer programs in the United States.

## The Fairness Doctrine had two basic elements:

- It required broadcasters to devote some of their airtime to discussion of controversial matters of public interest.
- to air contrasting views regarding those matters.

The doctrine did not require equal time for opposing views, but required that contrasting viewpoints be presented. If you think about what this doctrine accomplished it was to ensure that the news media presented enough information for individuals to reach their own conclusion regarding controversial issues. (Extensive coverage of this topic can be found in Wikipedia, the free encyclopedia, 6/21/2012 in the file titled: *Fairness Doctrine*, and in BSAlert.com in a file titled: *A Primer On The Fairness Doctrine: How We Screwed Up.*, 8/4/2012.)

You have heard the long-standing mantra of the conservatives that the media is biased toward the liberal viewpoint. I once heard a person state that the *Wall Street Journal* was too liberal for him. I believe the viewpoint about the liberal media including the *Wall Street Journal* is that they do present contrasting views and in doing so are judged to be liberal (read as unbiased). The conservatives had argued against the fairness doctrine for many years but court challenges had upheld this doctrine. When the wave of conservatism headed by Ronald Reagan and his followers hit Washington a conservative Reagan supporter was appointed head of the FCC and that board voted unanimously to abandon the fairness doctrine. In 1987 when Congress passed legislation to make the doctrine into a Federal law, Reagan vetoed the measure. Once the media was given free rein the outcome was conservative talk-show hosts who presented information as if it were factual when it was not. Also the onset of Fox News, which does not present news but presents the propaganda of the Ultra-Right, is a direct result of the revocation of the Fairness Doctrine. Whether such a doctrine could be enforced in today's world of media is not likely, but, the point remains that there was a systematic political philosophy espoused by the Republicans against there being an unbiased news source.

If you think back to the time when we saw Congress become so polarized it was very much about the time that the Fairness

Doctrine was removed and all regulation of the media was ended. The following are quotes from the WEB page of BSAlert.com.

"The repeal of the Fairness Doctrine harkened a new age in media and journalism . . ."

"Rush Limbaugh, Bill O'Reilly, Sean Hannity, Michael Savage and thousands of other partisan pundits were free to spews their slanted take on the world without . . ."

"Yes, the repeal of the Fairness Doctrine also gave liberal entities the same freedom. The problem is the platforms for these pundits were mostly commercial radio stations, and the conservatives took the role of the spokespeople for the agenda of corporate America . . ."

(http:bsalert.com//news/354/A_Primer_On_The_Fairness_Doctrine._How_We_Screwed_Up.)

Essentially the conservatives have the money and backing of corporate America which runs this country and the liberals do not have the resources or backing to offer a balanced presentation except for National Public Radio which is continually under attack by conservative Congress men and women who want to eliminate any public funding for this news source.


## Something missing here about compromise

Once the leaders of Congress could work together and in some situations work out a compromise. I do not know what happened to the idea of compromise, but rarely do we even hear the term and certainly do not see the outcome of a compromise. It seems that both the Democrats and Republicans have gotten stuck on the idea that to win is all that matters. When compromise was offered the stronger parties rejected it in favor of hate and revenge.

## Let's try consensus.

Wouldn't it be good for the Supreme Court to work on consensus as they deliberate an issue? In the book *The Poison Wood Bible* a missionary from America traveled to Africa with his family to carry the Christian message of Jesus to the natives. He was allowed to do what he wished, but the natives were wary of his ideas. At one point he became very angry as the natives would not go to the river to be baptized. He thought they were refusing to follow his teaching. He did not know that a young child had been killed by an alligator when she went near the river and thus the natives were afraid to go there. When issues arose in the congregation, the missionary wanted them to vote. The tribal chiefs had a style of working out issues in a group of the elders and they would talk and talk until they reached a decision that was accepted by the group. When one demands a vote, one divides the group into winners and losers. In a work to consensus, everyone wins. Perhaps we should encourage our newly elected representatives to travel to Africa and intern with a chieftain to learn the art of working for consensus. In the early days of America the Native Americans also used a system of compromise that the Europeans did not understand or respect and therefore ignored the process which might have led to less warfare.

The spate of talk-shows that tend to present material as if to inflame the listeners has little to do toward helpful solutions to our nation's problems. There seems to be no obvious way to bring persons to a reasonable manner of working to deal with issues that affect all of us. So long as our media continue to present material that is often inaccurate or based on limited information, we will continue to have an argument society.

# CHAPTER TWO

# THE DECLINE OF THE WEST
# IN WORLD AFFAIRS

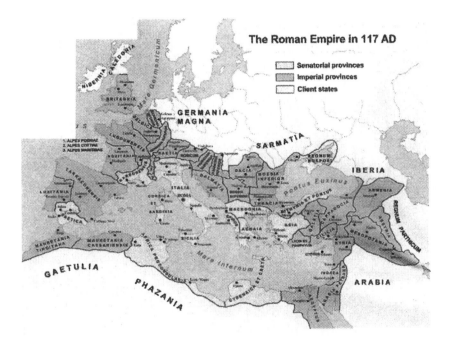

*The map above shows the Roman Empire at its zenith in 117 CE.
The influence of the Roman world has dominated western culture for
years but this dominance is being replaced by a broader world-view.
The Roman Empire was a relatively small part of the world making
up about one percent of the total land mass of the earth. The Empire
did contain roughly one-sixth to one-quarter of the human population
at that time. The influence of this Empire on our worldview has been
extensive, well beyond its borders.*

# What Has Happened to Western Civilization?

This may appear to be a rhetorical question, but it is meant literally. What happened to the core course in western civilization that was required of all college students at major universities in the early years of the 20ᵗʰ century? As a student at Stanford University, California, in 1958, I took what was normally a freshman course in my junior year as I was a transfer student. This was a powerful course with a huge reading list and sessions conducted by Teaching Fellows using a Socratic method. I remember the name of my teacher, Homer Chaney and I made certain to get him for all three quarters. Our reading list was comparable to the Harvard listing of major sources of knowledge called the Harvard Classics, but we did not study events before the early middle-eastern scholars who preceded the rise of the Greek and Roman cultures. We did learn about early religions in the area such as Zoroasterism and early law as the code of Hammurabi, but we did not stray beyond Babylonia thereby ignoring the vast areas of the world in Asia and Africa. The study of Western Civilization provided us with a unifying principle which held the American Europeans as the role model for all and gave us a common sense of superiority to other cultures. During the many conflicts in the U. S. centered on racial discrimination, the immigration of many people from other cultures, and our apparent racial wars in Asia and the Middle East, we lost the central focus of Europe and citizen groups like the Africans, Hispanics, and Asians were asking for alternatives to the course in Western Civilization. As a result the requirement that everyone take the standard, uniform course on Western Civilization was replaced by a series of alternatives to fulfill the world history requirement. However the replacement courses did not offer a unifying concept of our country, which left a gap in our socialization into American society. In a sense the Tea Party and gun lobby are the remnants of the myth of the domination of European-Americans in the U. S. and we have many citizens hailing from many nations and we have many religions that are alternatives to the Christian religion which was dominant in America in its earliest days of the massive migration of white, Europeans to this country.

For the western world, especially America, the cultural mix has changed in the last fifty years and European-Americans will become a minority group among a multicultural country where the Asians and Hispanics have become significant cultural groupings. This transition is neither good nor bad but is going to occur and we will have to adapt to many changes. We no longer should expect to have a Christian prayer before meetings of political groupings. We may have a prayer, but it must be acceptable to all. Freedom as we Americans have espoused it is not restricted to the European-Americans who came to this country and overwhelmed the native groups living here to establish America. However, it has taken us a long time to accept the Asians who came here to help build railroads in the West and stayed only to be segregated into special areas of our cities called China Towns. While the barriers have been lowered, those towns still exist. As a nation we have yet to acknowledge and ameliorate the conditions of the Native Americans we displaced to create the land of the free.

When Africans were put in chains and brought to the new world, we considered them to be property owned and used as we saw fit. While the reasons for America's civil war are many, it did take a war with massive loses for both the north and south to end slavery. Yet, with the formal end of slavery we still had a divided nation which took a second kind of war in the anti-segregation movement to break down the lasting barriers to racial integration. Following the end of the War Between the States several amendments to the Constitution were voted into effect with the 15th amendment prohibiting the denying of voting rights based on race. Yet one of the strongest supporter of voting rights, Charles Sumner of Massachusetts, abstained as the amendment did not restrict the use of other means to restrict voting such as a literacy test or poll taxes. For many years African-Americans were harassed if they tried to vote and it was not until 1948 that the United States military was integrated by President Truman.

There was gradual reduction in segregation which was strongly opposed by many Southern legislators and activists with continued harassment of African-Americans trying to register to vote or actually vote. The civil-rights movement eventually won out with school segregation discontinued and the elimination of white only coffee bars and restaurants although private clubs still did not accept Jewish people or African-Americans. At this date there is a renewed effort to block voting rights of minority groups by the arduous practice of requiring picture identification documents. For many this is not a serious situation but some elderly persons who cannot obtain a birth certificate are being denied the right to vote even when they had voted before. This is also a problem for new immigrants who may not have legal status in this country. There are active groups continuing to promote white supremacy in the face of the economic downturn and general dis-ease in of our country.

Now with the vast migration of Asians and Hispanics into America we have to face the reality that the old America envisioned in the course of Western Civilization can no longer be applied. Yet we have to find a unifying theme to help us re-identify America. We can find that theme if we understand that we are destined to be a multi-cultural country with no turning back.

## The myth of the melting pot

Just as we were exposed to Western Culture as our model, we were taught that our country was a melting pot. When I was in high school, this seemed to be true as the English, French, German, and Italian immigrants learned the English language and raised their children in Christian churches. However, the Jews always had problems assimilating into American life and the Hispanics were barely tolerated even though they were the backbone of agriculture in the southwest. The Jewish people seem to be accepted today and the African-Americans whose ancestors were forced to come here as slaves have slowly entered much of mainstream life in America. The newest immigrants that have yet to be accepted are the Asians where we still have China Towns in major cities, the Hispanics who still do much of the farm work in all states, and the Muslims who come here to work and live in America. But, their religions are foreign to us and conflicts have arisen over the construction of mosques in America. To keep the American dream alive we must extend all freedoms to all of our citizens. In the very early days of the migration of Europeans into American cities there was a sense of a melting pot in that most of these persons were from a similar cultural background and shared values. So long as the Africans were segregated from the "real" Americans we could maintain the lie that America was for Europeans. Even as the French gave us the Statue of Liberty as a reward for our accepting the many peoples from Europe, we forgot the message as it would be applied to non-Europeans who also wanted to share in the bounty of America.

The events during World War II were a major factor in breaking the barriers set up to segregate cultural groups such as the Jews and Africans as they joined in the goal of ending the war and bringing peace to the world. The aftermath of WW II was another reorganization of the world. America became the standard bearer for Western Culture and set up the North Atlantic Treaty Organization to defend the existing heartland. However, we became distracted when we shifted our focus to Korea and later to Vietnam. Not only did we stretch ourselves too far but we failed to accomplish the goals set prior to these military actions. While we were heady about the ends of World Wars I and II, we emerged from Korea and Vietnam as a wounded nation yet to fully heal.

We cannot go back to the good old days which I described as those of us born after the Depression and before World War II. We may be able to recall those days with fondness but we are subject to change and the world today is very different from what it was 50 years ago and we must accept those changes as inevitable and learn to live with all person as a community of equals.

America was built by immigrants who did not ask the natives for permission to come here and settle. We have continued to accept persons from other nations and have gained by these persons who come to work hard and to experience what we call the American Dream. We as a nation earned the Statue of Liberty from France because of our willingness to allow people to come to America and we need to re-new our commitment to that dream by offering a genuine alternative to the single-mindedness of what the course in Western Civilization taught with a modern philosophy which embraces all of our citizens.

# CHAPTER THREE

# THE HEARTLAND THEORY

### The Geo-political Organization
### of
### the World circa 1900

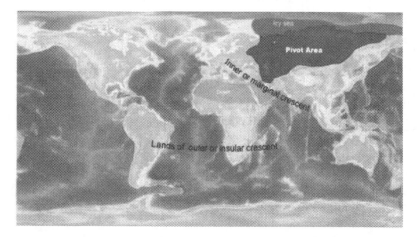

Colour representation, using a modem projection of the world.

*This map displays the Pivot Area for world dominance in Dark Green. It was this area that Europe must control to rule the world*

## The Heartland Theory

Very few of us have heard of the Heartland theory of geo-political world order. I first encountered this theory in 1954 when I was a junior naval aviator stationed at the Naval Air Station, Moffett Field, near Mountain View, California. Our commanding officer was a highly regarded Annapolis graduate who served in the Pacific on carriers in World War II. Traditionally we had an all pilots meeting every Friday at 1500 hours (3:00 P. M.). At one of these meetings our CO unfurled a map of the world and highlighted the core of European nations. He referred to a theory he probably learned as a midshipman at Annapolis or at the War College where officers slated for flag rank were given a clear message on the foreign policy of their country. When I left the Navy in 1956 and continued my college education at Stanford University I was required to take a year-long course in Western Civilization. There was no mention of this theory in our readings and I did not encounter the term until recently when I searched the inter-net and found several listings for the Heartland Theory. The one from which the pictures were taken was from Wikipedia.

In this theory the inner core of European nations was the area that ruled the world. Essentially it was offering the long-held notion that the European peoples were more advanced than other cultures as demonstrated by the colonization of most of Africa, America and Asia. The notion of superiority of the Caucasian Christians can be traced to the Roman Empire and later the Holy Roman Empire which held sway from the birth of Jesus of Nazareth into the 19th century. The Heartland Theory was the brain child of Halford John Mackinder who prepared an article for the Royal Geographic Society of England in 1904. He sorted out the world and gave a special status to Eastern Europe as the core in his theory. He divided the world into the World-island, the Offshore islands, and the Outlying islands.

The World-island was the core of the world and sat in control of the largest populations and the richest of all possible land combinations.

He placed emphasis on the land military rather than sea power and wanted to warn Britain that they should not try to rely on sea power as their major military force. Mackinder summarized his theory in 1919 with three specific statements.

- Who rules East Europe commands the Heartland;
- Who rules the Heartland commands the World Island;
- Who rules the World-Island controls the world.

If one looked at history, this theory seemed to be valid at that time. As early as Napoleon who planned to control the significant parts of the world believed he had to invade and defeat Russia in his endeavor. Later we find that European Nations gained control over India and China, colonized North and South America, and divided up Africa into enclaves. Even distant Australia and New Zealand came under the influence of Europe. The western European countries considered Russia as a large country that was difficult to rule and their government did not seem to be organized or effective. Russia did enter World War I very early but due to poor leadership and incompetent military commanders, Russia offered Germany a peace treaty only to give up their mother land to the communist regime. This was followed by bitter years of oppression by Stalin and his collaborators. World War II followed a similar pattern as World War I with Germany occupying France as a prelude to attacking Russia. The United States supported Russia in its war against Germany and eventually the Allies defeated Germany.

At the end of that war Eastern Europe was held together by a dictator named Tito who had a charmed life ensured by the European powers and the North Atlantic Treaty Organization, (NATO) dominated by the U. S. You can see the influence of this theory in the foreign policy of the European countries as during World War I the plan was for Germany to occupy France and then to turn on Russia to prevent it from incorporating the eastern European nations into its regime. This policy was the driving force behind Germany's tactics during the early days of World War II, but Germany was not going to get bogged down as in World War I in trench warfare and developed the concept of rapid advancement of the army with storm troopers supported by tanks and artillery. This worked well during the early years of the war. However, with support from the allies, Russia was able to stop the advance of the German army into the heart of Russia and eventually drove them back to Germany.

Following the end of the war, Europe was divided up into the western countries including the United States and the communist regime of the Soviet Union. The division became serious when the Russians took over many of Eastern European countries and built a wall to separate Eastern Germany (the German Democratic Republic) from Western Germany with its capital in Bonn as Berlin was within the Eastern region. America worked to develop a solid balance of power against the Soviet Union through the United Nations and the North Atlantic Treaty Organization (NATO). NATO was the watch dog to ensure that the heartland remained neutral or under European control. Note that Asia was not included in the heartland theory as an important area and at the time that theory was developed Europe dominated the world. When the United Nations was established the United States wanted to recognize the Nationalist Government of China led by Chiang Kai-shek that was based in Formosa which later was renamed as Taiwan. That viewpoint was maintained by America for many years excluding the large area of China under communist rule. In keeping with the heartland theory, mainland china was not important.

China was virtually ignored until the Korean War. The North Korean army crossed into South Korea and nearly overwhelmed the South. America, ill prepared for a new war, entered the conflict under a mandate by the United Nations and for some time there were various forces involved in the conflict. The U. S. forces did recover the southern part of Korea but continued northward to the Yalu River, the border between North Korea and China. The Chinese provided aircraft and pilots for the Russian MIG-15 jet fighters that flew against the bombing missions of the United States Air force. Just when it appeared the allies had won, Chinese troops swarmed into northern Korea pushing back the United States Marine and Army units. That story is well documented in many writings, but, no matter what the propaganda our government puts out, we lost the war in Korea ending up back at the 38th parallel which was the dividing line between the north and south set in 1945. The United States agreed to maintain a military presence in the south since the armistice which continues today. With our current worries about our length of stay in the Middle East, it is hard to imagine that our forces are still present in Korea many years after the end of the formal conflict.

In Europe Tito continued to rule the eastern European countries thereby ensuring that the Soviet Union could not control the heartland. The European powers tolerated Tito and supported his regime. But when Tito died there was a leadership void and the countries split up into competing nations and the old conflicts suppressed during the Tito regime re-emerged. Those conflicts went back to the time of the Ottoman Empire when Turkey controlled Eastern Europe. When that Empire dissolved the Turkish forces retreated but many Muslin families stayed in Europe. There always was a strong antagonism between the Christian and Muslin groups, and a virtual civil war broke out in the area. America encouraged NATO to work for peace and U. S. forces were used is some of the areas.

However, other areas of concern arose. For example, the shipping lanes along the east coast of Africa are dangerous with pirates capturing ships for ransom. The amount of money that was taken this way is unbelievable. But, the Nations paid as the captured ships were worth the price. Yet we must question how a poor nation like Somalia can harbor pirates who can humble the navies of the world as they attack and capture merchant ships almost at will. I wonder how many of our high school graduates know where the line from the Marine Hymn comes: "From the Halls of Montezuma and the shores of Tripoli." In 1895 pirates in northern Africa near Tripoli were capturing European shipping and we sent in the U. S. Marines to clear them out. It is doubtful whether the U. S. Marines could go in and remove the pirates from Somalia.

When the European countries moved out of their colonies the remaining nations were not divided along traditional boundaries and many civil conflicts have plagued the region. When England left India the Hindu and Muslin peoples had been held in check by the strict British rule but the major figure in the British withdrawal, Gandhi, was assassinated and India was divided along religious lines with Pakistan a Muslin state. In the attempt of the European nations to appease both sides they were allowed to maintain nuclear weapons in a mistaken attempt to balance the power of India and Pakistan.

We could go over the nations not in the Heartland to find examples where disputes abound. Sudan was not divided along tribal lines with years of conflict with the northern part constantly at war with the southern part. The borders in the Middle-east were drawn up rather arbitrarily and there was no identified country for the Palestinians. How could something that still keeps us in tension today have been allowed to occur if Britain had been thinking about peace. Of course, we saw from the British departure from India that they had not prepared the country for peace and that tension stills damages the U. S. today as we try to funnel supplies to our troops in Afghanistan through Pakistan.

We could continue with other examples, but it must be obvious that the theory of the Heartland is outdated and we need to develop a comprehensive view of the world with inter-related economies and cultures. It is this latter point that needs so much attention; can we truly accept the various cultures in our world into a single organization? Can the United Nations really work? These are questions to consider. The heart-land theory with Europe's core nations ruling afar is no longer valid. The old Soviet Union that was the balance to NATO led by Europe and America is no longer, and the internal dissent in the remaining Russia is strong. We have tried to maintain NATO as a viable force as with the first Iraq war where Bush senior and his chief diplomat James Baker did bring a cohesive force into Kuwait and Iraq only to leave before the full power of Saddam Hussein was blunted. In the next Iraq war we used NATO to maintain that we had multinational support for the war even though what support we had was at best only token. At this time NATO only serves to frighten Russia and to be a great drag on the U. S. economy. There is really no basis for U. S. forces to be billeted in any European country.

The important role of World War I in later world affairs can be seen from the material presented in the next section. It begins with a well-known poem by a U. S. soldier in the trenches of France followed by some comments on the events surrounding the war. This is followed by excerpts from an historical novel by Ken Follett about that war he called the *Fall of Giants*.

# World War I and Heartland Thinking

A well-known poem:

### *In Flanders Fields*

By Lieut.-Col John McCrae

In Flanders fields the poppies blow
Between the crosses, row on row,
That mark our place; and in the sky
The larks still bravely singing, fly
Scarce heard amid the guns below.

We are the Dead. Short days ago
We lived, felt dawn, saw sunset
glow, Lover and were loved, and
now we lie In Flanders fields.

Take up our quarrel with the foe;
To you from failing hands we throw
The torch; be yours to hold it high.
If ye break faith with us who die

We shall not sleep, though poppies
grow In Flanders fields.

# THE FOLLY OF THE GREAT WAR

# THE CAUSES OF WW I

H istorians have had a field day with World War I and its causes and outcomes. But the facts are that the conditions which led up to the war were present at a crucial juncture and once things began to happen, it could not be stopped until millions of young men had been killed and America belatedly entered the war with fresh troops overwhelming Germany who was forced to seek an armistice to end the war. David Stevenson has studied this war in great depth and I refer to his writings below. The pundits have pictured this war in many ways and a few of those pictorials are shown below.

"The Chain of Friendship", an American cartoon from 1914 depicting the web of alliances, captioned, "If Austria attacks Serbia, Russia will fall upon Austria, Germany upon Russia, and France and England upon Germany."

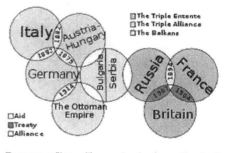

European military alliances shortly after outbreak of war

As David Stevenson has put it. "A self-reinforcing cycle of heightened military preparedness . . . was an essential element in the conjunction that led to disaster . . . The armaments race . . . was a necessary precondition for the outbreak of hostilities." David Herrmann goes further, arguing that the fear that "windows of opportunity for victorious wars" were closing, "the arms race did precipitate the First World War." If *Archduke Franz Ferdinand* had been assassinated in 1904 or even in 1911, Herrmann speculates, there might have been no war. It was" . . . the armaments race . . . and the speculation about imminent or preventive wars" that made his death in 1914 the trigger for wars. (From Wikipedia, *Causes of World War I*, 20 13.)

Germany, France, Russia, Austria-Hungary, and Britain attempting to keep the lid on the simmering cauldron of imperialist and nationalist tensions in the Balkans to prevent a general European war. They were successful in 1912 and 1913, but did not succeed in 1914.

## An interesting addendum to the Heartland Theory

Based on the book by Ken Follett titled the *Fall of Giants* published by Dutton Press in 2010 . . .

While working on this chapter I chanced upon a new book by Ken Follett. I have read many of his writings and have enjoyed his historical novels as I learn so much about history I never was taught in school. This book proved to be great one and it appeared as a synchronicity. When I opened the front cover, I was presented with a map of Europe which included the Heartland. I was duly stunned by seeing this map that was related to my writings. As I began to read this book I realized that the events which led up to WW I were driven by the Heartland concept. In fact one rarely can find a specific event which caused a major world event such as a war. There had been many small wars in this part of Europe for years and boundaries were constantly redrawn and those who lost territory and/ or status were angered while those who gained territory and/or status where haughty and arrogant which only made matters worse. The most significant event in this scenario was the visit to Serbia by the Archduke of Austria, Franz Ferdinand, in June of 1914. The Serbian leaders wanted to cause an event to bring about the formation of a new union in Eastern Europe. As the Archduke's visit was known in advance, persons were provided armament and training in their use with plans to assassinate the Archduke and his wife. One attempt involving a grenade was thwarted but a later attempt was successful as both the Duke and his wife were shot and killed.

This event might have been largely ignored except that Austria was angered and made several demands on Serbia which were unreasonable. They also set a deadline and when Serbia did not comply, Austria declared war against the small, defenseless territory of Serbia. As a result several other nations including Germany, France, Russia, and England, were unsettled and feared that the war might spread and began to prepare in that event. Once the mobilization of the military, especially by Russia who could amass a huge army on the border of Germany, and Germany which was militarily strong and would respond to the Russian mobilization it its mobilization of troops, it was essentially inevitable that a full scale war would result. The German high command had a long-standing tactic reflected in the Schlieffen Plan that called for attacking France through Belgium and to occupy France thereby releasing the German army to counter the attack by Russia which was assumed to be in the plans. We can see that the co-existence of the several powerful countries in Europe was tenuous at best and was so fragile that even the threat of the mobilization of Russia was enough to put Germany into a serious concern for her safety.

In essence the European countries were acting in accord with the roles assigned by the Heartland Theory. At this time the British considered themselves superior to any of the mainland countries although Germany was nearing equality. Britain had a treaty that it would send troops into France if Germany attacked. Germany believed it had no choice but to invade and occupy France if Russia declared war. In a sense there were several self-fulfilling prophecies that once in place would automatically proceed.

What happened was that Germany got embroiled in trench warfare in France that bogged down the troops for three years. Russia had the troops but poor organization and leadership as well as outdated weapons, and quickly negotiated a peace treaty with Germany. As the war dragged on, the leaders thought to get the major players into a meeting to end the war. When asked if they had achieved the goals of declaring war, no one answered. At this point they had forgotten the reason they went to war and now the only motivation for each was to win at all costs.

The saddest outcome of WW I was that it set up the conditions for a repeat performance in WW II. There was no real trigger for the war except that Serbia tried to enhance its image as part of the Heartland and Austria made demands and finally declared war. No one really won the war as the European nations had expended their young men in the prolong trench warfare. America was either lucky or Machiavellian by waiting until Germany was so weakened that they could not repel the influx of new, fresh troops. However America lost control over the peace process and Britain set up harsh demands on Germany and labeled them the cause and the loser of the war. The German people were given a crushing blow and the cost of reparations encouraged the German government to inflate their currency to pay off the debt. These two conditions, a people wanting to regain their self-image and to stop the economic destruction of their nation, they accepted Hitler's offer to redress these issues.

During the initial years of WW I Woodrow Wilson, President of the United States, stayed out of the war and began to develop a plan for a world-wide organization called The League of Nations. When it appeared to Germany that they were stalled in France, the German navy began using submarines to sink allied shipping which only served to tip the balance toward America sending troops to France. When the Americans entered the war they had fresh troops who were well fed and well-armed. The European countries had lost almost all of their able bodied youth to the war and America was able to overrun the Germans quickly. Eventually Germany realized that they could not prevail and sought a way to end the war. Early on the U. S. President and the British Prime Minister had hoped that the peace process would be gentle on Germany as Germany was no more responsible for the war than any other country. But the hard liners prevailed and Germany was hit with heavy demands for reparations. The war was formally ended by the Treaty of Versailles signed in 1919 to be effective January 10, 1920. The most damaging part of this treaty was that Germany was held to be solely responsible for the war. By now the Kaiser had abdicated his office; the Tsar of Russia was deprived of any power and eventually was murdered. The next German government was led by incompetent politicians and Russia was now a communist state. It might have been different if Wilson had remained healthy and had influence over the outcome, but the excessive reparations and striping Germany of its pride set up the conditions for the rise of a person like Hitler who promised to return Germany and her people to their former glory.

# SUMMARY

The heartland theory was a major factor in the foreign policy of the European nations up to and including World War II. Earlier Napoleon followed the idea that Europe needed to control Eastern Europe in order to control the world. This led him to a failed attempt to invade and pacify Russia. The heartland thinking of the German military was largely responsible for World War I as when Austria declared war against Serbia which would have lasted only a short time, Germany and Russia both mobilized troops. Germany followed the plan to invade and control France followed by a war against its major foe, Russia. The United States entered the war very late with fresh troops and was able to force Germany to seek an armistice which Woodrow Wilson supported, but England interfered with Wilson's plan for peace and placed severe conditions on Germany which setup the conditions for World War II. After that war America was at its zenith and developed NATO to contain the Soviet Union. Many of us lived through that period when the world was divided into the west led by the United States and Europe and the east led by the Soviet Union. The cold war was a war of testing and retesting the balance of power between the USA and the USSR which provided a form of peace.

Beginning with the failed war in Korea and later in Vietnam the United States lost its way and attempted to contain the Soviet Union and to encircle the East including China and Indochina. While the Soviet Union did fall apart, America also fell due to the costly wars and Europe got into a financial crisis as did the United States. One result of the costs of the Vietnam War was that America abandoned the Gold Standard in 1971. Co-jointly the eastern countries of Japan,

Korea, China, Vietnam, and India developed a strong economic base and were able to challenge the west for control of the world's economy, thereby negating the heartland theory of world control. We do not want another world war and this is a time to rethink our notion that the East is East and West is West and never the twain shall meet. This is a time to recognize that America is one among many nations and it is a time for us to come together in fusion.

One positive sign is the strong economic ties between nations and these ties will auger against military confrontations. Thus a form of fusion is in place and will increase to bring a sense of community to the nations of the world. In the global economy nations will become inter-dependent financially and war would be more or less avoidable.

# CHAPTER FOUR

# THE FALLACY THAT WE ARE NUMBER ONE

Jimmy Carter wrote: "Our nation has declared independence from the restraint of international organizations and has disavowed many long-standing global agreements, including judicial decisions, nuclear arms accords, controls on biological weapons, environmental protection, the international system of justice, and the humane treatment of prisoners. Even with our troops involved in combat and America facing the threat of additional terrorist attacks, we have neglected alliances with most of the very nations we need to have joined us in the long-term fight against global terrorism. All these political actions have been orchestrated by those who believe that the utilization of our nation's tremendous power and influence should not be constrained by foreigners. Regardless of the costs, some leaders are openly striving to create a dominant American empire throughout the world."

**From Jimmy Carter: *Our Endangered Values.***

## The rise and fall of the American Empire

There are many Americans who were born during the 1930s and those of us who were have a perspective on the status of America in the world order that is not shared by those born after World War II. We seem to be the decade of Americans who lived through the rise of America on the world scene with the outcome of the Second World War. We have also seen the decline in the status of America which began with the Korean conflict, the continued tension in Europe called the cold war, and then the debacle of the Vietnam War. We have labeled persons born after the war as the baby boomer generation. Perhaps we can label the newborns in the 30s as the Antebellum II generation—those born before WW II.

Let's review the experience of these Americans. America gained status with the war against Spain by which America gained territory and with the end of World War I where the U. S. entered the war belatedly with fresh troops and essentially brought the war to the point where Germany was forced to ask for an Armistice in 1917. President Wilson was crucial in this period, worked out a set of principles, and tried to form a League of Nations. He was distracted by personal events and Churchill dominated the post-armistice meetings whereby the Germans were treated as the defeated enemy and were forced to pay significant reparations. Wilson had wanted no reparations following the Armistice, and he was ignored by Britain, wanting to punish Germany with reparations including stealing their navy with the outcome setting up the conditions for the next war. The ending of the war was followed by a world-wide economic depression that doomed the Hoover administration and the Democrats led by Franklin Roosevelt came into office. America came out of the economic depression with massive help from the Roosevelt administration including the Tennessee Valley Authority whose effects are apparent today in the Southeast. One very significant program was Social Security to provide assistance for old-age persons enacted in 1935. We learned great lessons from the depression regarding borrowing too much money, investing in risky opportunities hoping to amass wealth, and adjusting our sights to meet our needs rather than our wants. Along with this experience, we watched a build up to war in Europe and the offensive by Germany into Poland and the Low Countries. Roosevelt awaited the attack by Japan on the U. S. Pacific battleship fleet in Hawaii before he was able to ask Congress to declare war on both Germany and Japan allowing him to send troops to Africa to aid his strong ally, Churchill, in his war to save the British Isles. That history is well documented with America overseeing the end of both the European and the Pacific wars and being the sole owner of the atomic bomb. This appears in retrospect to be the high point in America's standing in the world order. America was instrumental in forming the North Atlantic Treaty Organization (NATO) and establishing the United Nations which were major victories for the West. These were the heady days for the Americans with a booming economy and apparent world peace. That period of relief did not last very long.

We were ill prepared for the next two pivotal events—the Russian blockade of Berlin and the invasion of the South by North Korea.

In the summer of 1948 Russia blockaded Berlin which lay in the Russian sector of post-war Germany. As a response the United States organized an air-lift to provide supplies to Berlin as the rail and roadways as well as the canal passages to Berlin were closed. The airlift continued for several months until Russia agreed to reopen the corridor to Berlin. The second event occurred in 1950 when the North Koreans aided by China invaded South Korea. At the end of the Pacific war Korea was divided along the 38th parallel with North Korea under the control of China and South Korea under the control of America. America had reduced its military and was simply not ready for a new war. The United States, with assistance from the United Nations, hastily mobilized military units which did drive the North Koreans back above the 38th parallel, but when Chinese troops entered the war, they overwhelmed the U. S. forces and pushed them back to the original dividing line. The war turned into a stalemate with the result a negotiated truce re-establishing the 38th parallel as the boundary with a neutral zone as a buffer. The United States has maintained a presence in Korea with over 100 bases, roughly 30,000 military personnel at a cost of about 2 billion dollars a year.

These two events required America to expand its oversight into the East and cost America by having military units in Europe as a balance to the Soviet Union and in the East to defend Japan and keep South Korea in the America sphere of influence. The cold war in Europe drained America's treasury while the presence of China in the world order was a thorn in the side of America which did not recognize the independent status of mainland China for many years. Nevertheless, the United States was very watchful of the activities in the Far East and allowed itself to become embroiled in wars in Korea and Vietnam which ended in the withdrawal of American forces from that area. Belatedly America did recognize Communist China with the Nixon visit and later by admitting China to the United Nations.

There were several serious outcomes of the failed Vietnam venture including a divided home-land with protests against the war and the abandonment of the gold standard by the U. S. leading to worldwide inflation. The military draft was discarded and America's service men and women did not receive a warm welcome back home. The later military actions were a continued drag on the U. S. economy and continue today. I do not believe that those born before the Korean war were much affected by these events, but for those born later were greatly impacted by the Vietnam War and its consequences. The heady days of 1945 were never to return, and our current generations are rather negative and disappointed. What are some of the disappointments from the perspective of the antebellum II generation? I know that I speak for myself, but I believe others will share my views.

I truly believed that the hate of the McCarthy era would never return only to find the recurrence of that hate now expressed by the ultra conservatives and the Tea Party groups about immigrants, Hispanics, and Muslims. I had trusted that our leaders would remember the depression and not allow our economy to get out of balance as we did before. I heard the warning of Dwight D. Eisenhower about the military-industrial complex and to be ever careful to oversee that sector of our economy to avoid wasted billions on unnecessary military hardware. I had believed that we would foster education as a means of ensuring equality in the workplace and to overcome racial biases. Let us examine some of the areas of concern for me and move onto a means to working to recapture the good feelings of the Antebellum II generation and work toward a renewed interest in world harmony and world peace.

*William H. Calhoun, Ph. D.*

# Memories from an Antebellum II man

When I was an elementary school student we had special days for the birthday of Washington and Lincoln. I enjoyed those days and the names meant something to me as we studied about Washington as the father of our country and Lincoln as the president who saw the Union through a very bad time. I look with nostalgia to those days and they had meaning for us as we learned about America and its special place in the world. What happened to those days? Now we have President's day which has no special meaning for anyone. I guess it is a day for a generic president that we never learn about in school. I am rather selective in Presidents whom I admire, and I would like to honor those special ones.

I recall when I was a young man we celebrated Armistice day which we all knew was the celebration of that fateful day of 11-11-17 when World War I ended with peace in Europe and it was celebrated when the troops came marching home. Today on November 11th, we celebrate Veteran's day, which is as neutral and generic as President's day, and has no special meaning for most of us. I am a veteran but I do not put out a flag or go to any parade as it just does not have any meaning for me.

Today when I see military persons on television I am appalled at the huge spread of ribbons on their chests. When I was a Naval Office the rules were that one never wore more than nine ribbons, which yielded a three by three square. Ribbons were individual and each was pinned on. Today I see a whole spread of ribbons in numbers over thirty and I cannot help to think that these ribbons have lost any meaning by their sheer numbers. Recently I attended a ceremony where I was shocked to see that the ribbons were made of plastic rather than individual ones and I guess you just went to the local base store and listed what you had and a plastic sheet of the ribbons was prepared for you. I served in the Navy for four years and I had one ribbon. I recall a senior aviator who had a Navy Cross for his bombing mission in the Pacific during World War II and that was his only ribbon. But he wore it with pride and we all knew what it was—a Navy Cross.

Once military personnel did not leave the base dressed in utilities. They were expected to present a good image in proper uniform at all times. A good sailor always had on a hat, or as we said, was covered, and did not put his hands in his pockets. Today it is nothing to see personnel on the street in utilities or what we now call camies (camouflage uniforms) without a hat and hands in the pockets. I will leave this issue without further comment.

## What is the true status of America on the world scene?

We often hear comments that we are the greatest nation in the world. This is a false statement but perhaps a dream, but we are only one among many. With the end of World War II when we were self-appointed victor in the two World Wars and only America had the Atom bomb, we could think of ourselves as on top of the world, but things have changed. There was a long standing fallacy that we never lost a war. We just did not count the War of 1812. We did not win the war in Korea and we still have a major military force defending South Korea. We tried to maintain control of nuclear weapons, but with time that control was lost and cannot be regained. One of the biggest blows to our status was to admit that mainland China did exist and did deserve to be in the United Nations. We also were fooled to think that our technology could be equal to an overwhelming ground force in South East Asia and had to exit that war as a clear loser. It was during the Vietnam War that America left the gold standard and let its currency inflate to pay for the war. This event resulted in a world-wide recession which is rarely acknowledged.

## Even though we have the largest military in the world, we cannot rule it

We do have the largest military force in the world but at a huge cost to the economy. We have 700 or more military installations world-wide in at least 100 countries. However, as Paul Rasor pointed out, our military leaders appear to have forsaken their role in defending the United States and instead are fostering a drive for empire (Paul Rasor, *Reclaiming Prophetic Witness*, 2012). We would be wiser to spend money on our infrastructure than on F-22s that provide little more than a claim that we have the best and most expensive military aircraft in the world. In fact, the F-22 has proved to be a lemon of a plane as pilots do not want to fly in it and there are persistent problems with the oxygen system the U. S. Air Force has tried to hide and later to fix. In considering these costs, the data show that the F-22 program cost the U. S. tax payers over 86 billion U. S. dollars and the cost of a single plane delivered to the Air Force costs 150 million. Imagine what we could do to the federal debt if that program had not been funded by Congress? We usually recoup some of the costs by selling aircraft to foreign countries, but the Military has banned the sale of the F-22 abroad, presumably due to the problems the plane has had. We have become, rather than a respected nation, through our actions in the Middle East and elsewhere, a bully nation.

Berkeley Bedell (*Revenue Matters*, 2011) noted that in the last ten years we have lost more soldiers than any other nation, we have killed more civilians with our military might than all other nations, and we have helped to create a group of persons committed to our destruction because of these actions. One presidential candidate asked us to be a kinder and gentler nation. I believe we should ask the same of our nation today.

Many Americans proudly proclaim that America is number one. In some respects this may be true. We have the largest economy in the world and the largest military of any country. The United States has produced the largest number of highly acclaimed movies. But this is not enough to give us the outright lead.

Now, by contrast, let us determine where we are No. 1 in places that are not admirable.

- We have the highest rate of sentencing people to prison of all nations and we have the largest prison population of any other country.
- We have the largest percentage of obese persons than any other country.
- We have the highest divorce rate, the most hours of watched television, and the highest rate of illegal drug use. The latter in spite of our "War Against Drugs."
- We have more car thefts than any other country, the highest percentage of reported rapes, reported murders, and the highest percentage of crimes.
- We also have the largest police force than anywhere else in the world.
- We have the largest health-care costs per Gross Domestic Product of all the countries in the world, we have the largest

      percentage of persons taking prescription medication, and the largest percentage of women taking anti-depressant medications.

- America's college students have the highest amount of debt for education of all other nations.

- We spend seven times for our military than any other nation, and we have the largest national debt of all.


## How do we do in the Olympic Games?


The Olympic Games originated in Greece in a valley named Olympia in 776 BCE. These games were very important at that time and brought city-states together to compete in a less harmful way than war. The games were scheduled every four years until banned in 393 A.D. Europeans were responsible for the resurrection of the Olympic Games in 1896 and they have continued to today with a rotation among nations. French and German teams of scientists worked to unearth the old site of the games in Greece and were active in restarting the games.

    The United States has generally scored well in the Olympic Games, although it is important to give credit to the many African-Americans who have run under the U. S. flag. In the 1920 summer games the U. S. won 95 medals, which include Gold, Silver, and Bronze. The 1936 summer games were held in Berlin and the U. S. had to remove several Jewish athletes although one black track star did compete. Germany won the most medals with 89 while the U.S. won 56. Generally the leaders have been China, the Soviet Union (later Russia, and even later the United Team of 15 former Soviet Republics), and the United States. There are two interesting events in this history. There was a young black man born in Alabama whose family later moved to Cleveland, Ohio where J. C. Owens was given the name of Jesse by a school teacher who misunderstood his strong southern accent. Jesse began a career in track and field in high school and was able to attend Ohio State University. He trained for and was selected to compete for the United States in the summer Olympics of 1936 in Berlin, Germany. In that set of games he won four gold medals by winning the 100 and 200 meter races, the long-jump, and as one of four members of a 400 meter relay race. It was reported that Hitler stormed out of the stadium when an African-American won gold medals.

The second story is very similar in the Joe Louis Barrow (The Brown Bomber) was also born in Alabama and his family moved to Detroit during what was termed the great migration. He began training for boxing at an early age and began to win. Again we have an African-American in the spot light and a fight was arranged for New York City in 1936 at the Yankee Stadium with Max Schmeling, who was an outstanding boxer for Germany. Louis lost only three fights in his career but he did lose to Schmeling in the 12th round of the fight. Schmeling returned to Germany to great ovations. A rematch was arranged and was again in Yankee Stadium. This fight lasted only two minutes and two seconds. Louis came out hitting and decked Schmeling with vicious punches, thus redeeming himself in the eyes of his fans.

There are several areas where we are number one but that does not mean we are good or bad. You will have to read these comments and determine what you think. We are the number one nation in edible exports, meaning that we export more food items to other countries than any other single country. We are number one in the importation of animals, either alive or for food, sugar, and paper.

We are also number one for the amount paid for health care as a total and per capita as was noted above. Canada is rated to have one of the best health-care systems with a rating of 17-19 while America's rating is 54-55. Cuba has the highest rating of all the Caribbean nations and surpasses the United States with a rating of 23-25. That came as a shock to me as we belittle Cuba greatly and assume it is doing badly.

One interesting rating is the percentage of persons in a country who accept evolution as a viable theory of the origin of the species. America is next to last with about 27% reporting acceptance of the theory. Iceland is number one and Turkey is the only nation with a lower percentage than America. I would conclude that our educational system is failing to teach a balanced view of science, and especially the study of the origin of the species. Regarding education, the United States has slipped in its rankings scoring about average in the areas of mathematics, reading, and science. American students received a score of 487 (of a total of 1000) in math, 500 in reading, and 502 in science. There is an argument that America need not worry about education as immigrants from other nations come to America and bring with them high educational achievement. For example, in the Hitler period many Jewish families migrated to America and among that group where a number of scientists who would greatly add to America's standing in the world. These scientists helped the United States advance nuclear science and in the advancement of our space program. However we cannot assign the responsibility for America's educational system to an influx of non-Americans.

Perhaps one major area where America is clearly not number one is the Happy Planet Index and the Peace Index. The Happy Planet Index is an estimate of the human well-being and environmental impact introduced by the New Economics Foundation in 2006. This measure is offered as an alternative to other common measures of a nation's health such as the GDP and the Human Development Index. You will have to make whatever you want from this information, but this is one more measure that may be useful in the planning by nations for change. In spite of what we consider poverty, the Caribbean nations rank very high. Among the five nations with the largest economies the highest rankings on the Happy Planet index is Japan at 45, Germany 46th, France 50th, and China 60th, while the United States was only 105th.

A somewhat similar measure of the status of a nation is the Global Peace Index. This measure was developed by the Institute for Economics and Peace and was first started in 2007. Currently it ranks 158 nations on its index and was the brain child of Steve Killelea of Australia and it is endorsed by several leading personages including the Dalai Lama, Desmond Tutu, Jeffery Sachs, and Jimmy Carter. This index is based on a number of factors such as the number of wars fought, political instability, the level of violent crimes, the number of persons in jails, and the export of weapons. Of the 158 nations included, Iceland had the highest ranking of Number 1. The United Kingdom was 29th, Brazil 83rd, and the Unites States 88th.

The personal belief that we are number one among nations is highly subjective and based on information from many sources. What I have tried to do in this section is to present a variety of data and facts that can be amassed to evaluate the status of America as a member of the community of nations in our world. We clearly have high status regarding our economy and our military institutions. We fall down when one examines our expenses for health-care, and in a variety of other measures such as the number of persons in jails, the occurrence of violent crime, and the rate of mental illness as accessed by the use of legal and illegal drugs. Our performance in education is only average at best and most striking is that most people do not accept evolution as a viable theory regarding the origin of the species. We also are a nation of people who are not very happy, in spite of our affluence, and we are not a nation of peace. One finding worth noting is that rich countries also have the largest group of impoverished people as the money becomes the property of the rich.

# CHAPTER FIVE

# OUR FAILED ECONOMIC SYSTEM

*SLOWLY*          *I'M*

*GOING*          *FOR*

*DOWN*          *SALE*

America's World Standing          How Congress See Themselves

**"***At the root of America's economics lies a moral crisis: the decline of civic virtue among America's political and economic elite. A society of markets, laws, and elections is not enough if the rich and powerful fail to behave with respect, honesty, and compassion toward the rest of society and toward the world. America has developed the world's most competitive market society but has squandered its civic virtue along the way. Without restoring an ethos of social responsibility, there can be no meaningful and sustained economic recovery."* (From *The Price of Civilization* by Jeffery D. Sachs, 2011.)

Jeffery Sachs is an internationally known economist who is an expert in helping countries solve economic problems through a practice he described as clinical economics. Sachs acknowledges that he was fortunate in being able to study economics with intellectual giants who had done much to guide America's economic path following World War II. One major giant was Paul Samuelson who wrote the basic text on economic theory used for many years. Sachs wrote that the period of the 1940s to the 1970s could rightly be called the Samuelson Era in economics. From Samuelson, Sachs gleaned the following five basic ideas (Sachs, *The Price of Civilization*, 2011, page 28).

- Markets are reasonably efficient institutions for allocating society's scarce economic resources and lead to high productivity and average living standards.
- Efficiency, however, does not guarantee fairness (or "Justice") in the allocation of incomes.
- Fairness requires the government to redistribute income among the citizenry, especially from the richest members of the society to the poorest and most vulnerable members.
- Markets systematically under provide certain "public goods," such as infrastructure, environmental regulation, education, and scientific research, whose adequate supply depends on the government.
- The market economy is prone to financial instability, which can be alleviated through active government policies, including financial regulation and well-directed monetary and fiscal policies.

Sachs believes that the economic crisis in America began with the Vietnam War when the Bretton Woods dollar exchange system collapsed, mainly due to the inflation of the U. S. dollar to pay for the Vietnam War. One outcome was the abandonment of the gold standard by the United States in 1971. America's economic policies during the Vietnam War were destabilizing to the world economy. The resulting crisis in the world economy ushered in a period of distrust of the mixed economy championed by Samuelson and led to the revision of many policies during the Reagan and Thatcher years. The main effect of this event was not that specific but led to an antipathy regarding the role of government in economic policy which resulted in a near abandonment of the poor who relied on government help and opened the doors to the rich to shed their moral responsibility to the rest of society.

## From *Revenue Matters* by Berkeley Bedell we quote:

*"In terms of financial wealth, the top ten percent of households have 38.3 percent of all privately owned stock, and 62.4 percent of business equity. The top 10 percent have 80 percent to 90 percent of stocks, bonds, trust funds and business equity, and over 75 percent of non-home real estate. Since financial wealth is what counts as far as the control of income-producing assets, we can say that just 10 percent of the people own the United States of America."* (Bedell, P. 6.)

Berkeley Bedell is known by most as the owner of a fishing tackle business which he started at a young age. He also served in the Army Air Corps during World War II as a flight instructor. He received recognition as the National Small Business Person of the year in

1964 by President Lyndon Johnson. In 1970 he became disillusioned with the Vietnam War and complained to his congressman. When the congressman did not listen to Bedell, Bedell ran as a Democrat in a heavily Republican district in Northwestern Iowa in 1979 and won 49 percent of the vote. He ran again in 1981 and won the seat where he served for 12 years. His recent book reflects his experience as a business person and congressman and brings attention to the state of the United States economy. He subtitled that book:

## *Tax the rich and restore Democracy to save the nation.*

Some of the wisdom from his 90 years on this earth, Bedell wrote the following.

- Show me a business that ignores revenue and focuses only on cutting costs and I will show you a business that is headed for failure.
- Show me a government that ignores revenue and focuses only on cutting costs and I will show you a government that is a failure.
- Show me a business that only cuts back and does not charge forward and I will show you a business that is headed for failure.
- Show me a government that only cuts back and does not charge forward and I will show you a government that is a failure.

Returning to Sachs, he wrote that he had finished his work for the PhD in Economics and joined the faculty at Harvard in 1980. He was very fortunate to study the great economists of America including Adam Smith and Paul Samuelson. But, by contrast, this also was the year that Ronald Reagan was elected to the White House on a platform of ". . . rolling back government the likes of which had not been seen in decades." Reagan had the skill and experience to present his proposals with confidence and in a mannerly way. As noted above, ten percent of the population of America actually own America, and when this ten percent were given tax cuts and when many businesses were freed for regulation, the downward spiral of the United States economy accelerated.

## Prosperity lost

Chapter 2 of Sachs book is titled Prosperity Lost and that chapter began with the following.

"There can be little doubt that something has gone terribly wrong in the U. S. economy, politics, and society in general. Americans are on edge, wary, pessimistic, and cynical."

Referring back to the earlier chapter where I cited the experience of those born before World War II who had seen a gradual improvement in the life situation as we overcame the depression with many federal programs, entered a war for which the nation was fully prepared and which in fact was short in comparison with later wars such as Vietnam and in the Middle-east. Service personnel returning home found jobs, educational benefits, and a strong Veterans' Administration offering medical care and home loans. Even with the war in Korea we did not lose our sense of wellbeing, although we were ill prepared for that war which ended in a draw.

Sachs is mostly referring to those citizens born after the Korean War or later who have seen a gradual reduction in the quality of life in the United States which was markedly accelerated with the conservative Republicans taking over the White House in 1985. With an ally in David Stockman, Reagan had promised to reduce spending by the government to reduce the national debt and to provide tax relief for the general population. When in office Reagan reneged on his pledge and did not cut programs if his friends protested although he did reduce taxes. From this perspective, a large number of the citizens saw the government as a group of individuals interested in their special interests and the interests of their friends in business who were the basis for the donations to fund future campaigns for re-election. Sachs believed from his experience that most citizens saw big business and government working together for goals which not only ignored the needs of consumers and investors, but actually worked to damage consumers and investors.

I am old enough to remember the fateful words of D. D. Eisenhower in his farewell speech January 17, 1961 when he spoke:

## "Beware the military-industrial complex."

President Eisenhower was warning us that the strong lobbyists for military budgets coupled with the cozy relations of those lobbyists with big business, the military had a great advantage over most other agencies seeking funding for programs. Recall the cost of the F-22 program which was pushed through Congress in spite of concerns from the Military about the program.

Those of you who have studied history may remember the earlier cry about the military-industrial complex offered by Harry S Truman.

Truman had served with the artillery during World War I and had been elected to the Senate from Missouri in 1934. During his first term he spoke out against Wall Street greed and the dangers of unrestricted capitalism. Later he traveled to several military bases where he encountered waste and poor management. He was able to establish what was later called the Truman Committee to investigate waste in military spending.

---

## THE TRUMAN COMMITTEE OF WORLD WAR II

Truman as Senator had received complaints about waste in our military buildup for entry into World War II. When he visited Fort Wood in Missouri he found that employees who had no job responsibilities were still being paid, expensive equipment and supplies were not used but deteriorated, and many contractors worked on a cost plus basis. (*Truman*, by David McCullough, Touchstone, NY 1992.)

---

One of the worst examples of profiteering from war appropriations was that of the Curtis-Wright firm which knowingly allowed faulty aircraft engines to be installed. The Army Air Corps denied any problems but one General was sent to jail for his role in this program. Truman did use his role on this committee to enhance his image with the White House; he did a great service for the country. He too, like Eisenhower, warned of the conspiracy of the military with big business to funnel huge amounts of money for military programs with little if any oversight.

It is obvious that most politicians have failed to heed the warning by Eisenhower about the powerful lobbies and the contributions to run campaigns for office. It is also obvious that David Stockman was very conservative but he also had a sense of ethics that most politicians lack. Yet his message was ignored, as with the recent Supreme Court's ruling that a corporation can make contributions for the making of advertisements by political candidates. The court also removed the restriction on the timing of advertisements regarding elections. This ruling was another example of the polarization of our government into extremes with a five of nine votes by the judges determining the outcome.

In another era we found a similar warning, but this time from a conservative republican David Stockman. As mentioned above, Reagan had asked David Stockman to head his team to develop an economic plan to reduce government spending and to lower taxes. Stockman was born in Texas in 1981 to parents of German descent. His family was conservative and a grandfather had been active in the Republican Party for many years. Stockman received a B. A. from Michigan State University in 1968. He studied economics at Harvard from 1968 to 1970 and later attended Harvard Divinity School in 1974-75. He served in the House of Representatives from 1977 to 1981 from Michigan and Director of the Office of Management and Budget (OMB) 1981-1985. In many ways Stockman was an idealist as he also spent time at Harvard Divinity School, hardly typical of a conservative republican. He drew plans for the Reagan administration but once Reagan was in office he proceeded to ignore those plans as in Stockman's words, "Reagan could not say no to a friend who came asking for money." The result was the government spending remained high while taxes were cut causing an increase in the federal debt. Stockman was asked to be interviewed by a correspondent from *The Atlantic Monthly* and the interview was published as "The Education of David Stockman." In this interview he was blunt and forthcoming. He indicated the weaknesses of Reagan's fiscal skills and essentially dug himself a deep hole. His influence was weakened and he resigned the Directorship of OMB in 1985. He later published a book which laid out the failings of the Reagan administration in detail. Once again the politicians ignored the warnings of Stockman about the supply-side economic theory.

The next case of a failure to heed the past was when Dick Cheney was Vice President under George W. Bush. Shortly after Bush took office he was able to push through a major tax code revision reducing the revenue especially from the richest group of tax payers. The result was another large increase in the deficit. At that time Paul O'Neill was the Secretary of the Treasury and he warned Cheney about the mounting deficit indicating it was a problem. Cheney was quoted as telling O'Neill "You know, Paul, Reagan proved that deficits don't matter." One month later Cheney fired O'Neill to replace him with John Snow, while Snow persisted in saying that deficits do matter.

Sachs ended this chapter with a plea for honesty and responsibility by the rich for not ignoring the plight of the poor.

"Our challenges lie not so much in our productivity, technology, or natural resources but in our ability to cooperate on an honest basis. Can we make the political system work to solve a growing list of problems? Can we take our attention away for short-run desires long enough to focus on the future" Will the super-rich finally own up to their responsibilities to the rest of society? These are questions about attitudes, emotion, and openness to collective actions more than about the death of productivity or the depletion of resources." (Page 25.)

## Mindfulness

Where does mindfulness enter our picture of economic failure? Think of the paragraph above in which Sachs mentions the short-run desires that seem to control so much of our society. People will stand in line for hours to purchase the latest gimmick produced by Apple or Amazon, just to show that they have the latest in technology. Persons will purchase a vehicle such as the Hummer which consumes gasoline like none other, just to show off to his or her peers, ignoring the waste of fuel this produces. The city mileage of 14 miles per gallon is not that much worse than many large pickup trucks, but the Hummer performs poorly on the highway with an MPG of 18 when many modern automobiles can get 30 MPG on the highway and some of the hybrids can reach 60 MPG. The Hummer stands out as an ego vehicle for men and sadly women who want to show off their misuse of their resources.

Sachs spends most of chapter writing about how distracted we are as a culture. To be mindful is to be aware of what we are doing and why. But when persons will walk in the park with ear buds that block out the sounds of wildlife and water, they are not aware of where they are or what they are doing; they are not being mindful. When students on campus walk among the trees and lawns of the university with a cell phone glued to their ears, they are not aware of the world around them. They are missing out on much of life. As a nation we spend more time watching television than any other country. But there is so little on television that has any depth of meaning. When a movie is judged by its special effects and loud sounds rather than its depiction of the human condition, we have forgotten what movies are to be about. Along with the distraction of the media to our lives, we have also forgotten the role that the family plays in the lives of its members. We hear politicians speak of family values but I have yet to hear one explain what such values mean. Several years ago I read an analysis of the tests students complete when applying for National Merit Scholarships. One significant factor among the recipients of the award was that they met together to share the evening meal. That to me is a significant family value. When we put so much emphasis upon ensuring that our children have the latest name-brand clothing rather than what they have for breakfast, we lose a family value.

Major distractions in our culture are the excessive advertisements by the drug industry in magazines and on television. A second distraction is the repeated advertisements by lawyers saying they can get you money if you are injured, they will get you Social Security disability status, etc., etc. The role of advertising in our culture is to create a sense of need for items which are not actually required. Many years ago families used their resources to meet their needs for food, shelter, clothing, and medical care. Today we are not only motivated to meet our needs, but we now try to meet our wants. Professionals who council family members in debt find that most persons will not cancel their cell phone contract to save money. The comment is: "I need to have my cell phone." No, they do not need their cell phone. That is a want. A side effect of our advertising and fast-food life style has resulted in marked increase in obesity, diabetes, and related health issues. The United States population has more obese persons than any other nation and obesity is predicted to reach fifty percent in a few years. The United States is the most highly commercialized nation in the world, and as Sachs points out, the highly commercialized countries tend to have the highest rate of poverty. "Whatever the cause, the United States is privately rich but socially poor." That point might relate to our tendency to be unhappy with the state of our world. We have money but we do not use it wisely and for the common good of all.


## The Crisis in Higher Education

Very similar to the housing market in the United States a few years ago before the collapse of the home sales market, higher education is on the edge of a great fall. The cost of tuition at all universities, especially the comprehensive universities, has risen at rates higher than the cost of living. As a graduate of Stanford University (The Leland, Jr., Stanford University) in 1959 I can present it as an example without meaning to single it out as it is typical of the upper tier of private universities. From the table on the next page, you can see that the tuition has risen dramatically from a low of $600 dollars in 1950 to a high of nearly $40,000 in 2012. The growth rate of tuition is accelerating beyond sustainable levels. Most university officers will cite the mantra that most students do not pay the full cost as there are fellowships and scholarships available. Even in that case, the rate of increase in actual costs of higher education is still much too high, well beyond the rise in the cost of living.

What drives this rise in cost? The great halls of learning have been corrupted by the capitalist model used by business to a fault. They have maintained that they must pay University Presidents salaries equivalent to that of CEOs in business to attract high quality personnel. At one time the honor of being a university president was considered a major part of the payment for presidents. D. Eisenhower accepted the role of President at Columbia upon completion of his stint as President of the U. S. That was quite an honor at that time.

# THE EXPONTIAL RISE IN COLLEGE TUITION

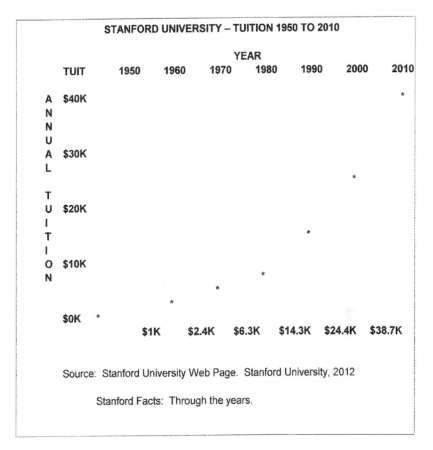

STANFORD UNIVERSITY – TUITION 1950 TO 2010

Source: Stanford University Web Page. Stanford University, 2012

Stanford Facts: Through the years.

Today university presidential candidates apply widely for positions and often move to several different positions during their life time and they seem to be more concerned about remuneration than loyalty to their institution.

The student loan program which is backed by the U. S. government is partly the cause of the massive increases in tuition. As home buyers were induced to take out huge loans to buy their dream home, students are borrowing large amounts to attend the college of their choice. When I attended Stanford I was married and owned a small home in Mountain View, California. The tuition was

$750 in 1956-57 and I had the G. I. Bill and could easily handle the finances. As a college professor I always told students not to borrow money to go to college. I usually was speaking to students applying to graduate school, but now I find that families are going in debt for undergraduate education. The saddest thing about all of this is that modern college degree programs rarely prepare students for a viable career. This is especially true in the liberal arts areas that do not include useful internships during the student's education. The most recent data suggests that one out five families have borrowed money for one or more children to attend college. One thing the students do not do is plan ahead. As soon as they graduate the collection agency is at the door asking for a payment. This is the time when students are least able to start repaying their debt but they signed documents stating they would repay on time. One sad commentary on the American way is that students get the impression that they will not have to repay the loans as the Federal Government will forgive them the debt. Sadly, this is false. The prediction from these data is that colleges and universities will suffer a serious collapse in the financial health as tuition cannot continue to increase as it has in the last 20 years.

## How does mindfulness apply here?

Jeffery D. Sachs offers a Path to Prosperity in Part II of his book. He introduced the topic stating that the problems of America begin at home, and with the choices and decisions each of us are making in our lives. "The relentless drumbeat of consumerism into every corner of our lives has led to extreme shortsightedness, consumer addictions, and the shriveling of compassion." We are so distracted by this state of being that we have allowed the power that should be ours to be usurped by lobbyists. "As a society, we need to establish the right relationship of markets, politics, and civil society to address the complex challenges of the twenty-first century." He does not brush this off with the idea that there is a simple solution such as smaller government, more de-regulation, or less freedom for individuals. These are complex challenges. He also argued that the future does not belong to the Tea Party, but to the youth who are the most progressive and diverse part of our society.

## The middle path

As Sachs quoted:

"Two of the greatest ethicists in human history, Buddha in the East and Aristotle in the West, hit upon a remarkably similar prescription for the long-term happiness of humanity. 'The Middle Path," said Buddha in the fifth century BCE, would keep humanity balanced between the false allures of asceticism on the one side and pleasure seeking on the other side. Two centuries later and half a world away, Aristotle gave his fellow Greeks a similar message, that "moderation in all things" was the key to *eudemonia*, human fulfillment." Yet, we find the middle-path of Buddha and Aristotle as a way is challenged by both the libertarianism of the free-market, conservative members of society, as well as some ultra-conservative politicians.

For Sachs, mindfulness means an alertness and quiet contemplation of our circumstances, putting aside greed and distress. As the Buddhists say, being mindful allows us to gain insight into ourselves and to escape from endless craving for more. There is a parallel notion of those who find that they have enough for a good life and those who believe they will never have enough regardless of their wealth and accumulations.

Sachs specifically lists eight areas where we ought to be mindful.

- *Mindfulness of self:* personal moderation to escape mass consumerism.
- *Mindfulness of work:* the balancing of work and leisure.
- *Mindfulness of knowledge:* the cultivation of education.
- *Mindfulness of others:* the exercise of compassion and cooperation.
- *Mindfulness of nature:* the conservation of the world's ecosystems.
- *Mindfulness of the future:* the responsibility to save for the future.
- *Mindfulness of politics:* the cultivation of public institutions.
- *Mindfulness of the world:* the acceptance of diversity as a path to peace.

## Needs versus wants

Many years ago many families knew what they needed to survive in moderate happiness. We need work to earn an income, a home or residence, food, nutrition with balanced meals to provide the basic chemical needs of the body, love to have and to give, clothing, a means of transportation, and a few other items. As Sachs quoted, basic survival goods are cheap. However, narcissistic self-stimulation and social-display products are expensive. When was the last time you saw an advertisement for Viagra whether male or female and the last time you saw an advertisement for an SUV, a HUMMER, or a

Porsche? These are clear examples of narcissistic self-stimulation or social-display. Yet many of the items that Americans crave are not openly advertised such as illegal drugs and pornography.

One of the most difficult areas for mindfulness is concern for others. We cited information earlier that most rich countries have the largest group of poor. We Americans fit that model. Our poor are suffering while we ship more edible food items overseas that any other nation. Daily we hear how conservative politicians want to reduce or eliminate the safety net we have for our poor. I will wager that in every family there will be at least one person who is unable to function in our society due to mental illness or some other debilitating factor. Using that as a base line, can we be mindful of our unfortunate family member while ignoring all the others?

A mindful society is not a specific plan, but an approach to life that allows us to live without being driven by our unlimited wants. Imagine if you attended a football game and rooted for both sides. Maybe our stress on competition in sports is hurting us as we find teams that are rewarding players who intentionally injure other players. We even find this behavior in little-league and the like. We often hear that we have college sports to teach sportsmanship. Let us be mindful of that goal. Real sportsmanship teaches one to honor the other players and to treat them with respect. That is what being mindful is about.

# CHAPTER SIX

# WHAT IS THE ROLE OF
# OUR MILITARY?

The F-22                                    Raptor in Flight

USS Ronald Reagan

C an we actually be in charge of the world?
Although America spends billions for its military operations world-wide, we have failed to bring peace to the world. It may be that our military has lost sight of the goal of defending America at its borders to adopting a strategy which is designed to build an empire for America. As we have seen in our history books that countries that tried to build an empire eventually failed because such an endeavor could not be sustained due to the costs and demands on the military to operate on foreign shores. Currently of all the money spent on military operations of all nations in the world, America accounts for

thirty-nine percent of that total. In this chapter we will examine how well our money is being expended in our endeavors toward an empire and speculate whether that empire can be acquired and sustained.

Reviewing some of the figures for our budget, for the Fiscal Year 2010 the total defense budget reported by the government was $682 billion dollars. Forty-one percent of this amount was for operations and maintenance. A like amount was for research and procurement of new weapons systems. The Department of Defense accounted for roughly twenty percent of the total budget. That amount needs to be qualified as there are funds being funneled to the military that do not appear in this category. When we examine individual systems later, you will find that costs are truly hard to pin down to exact amounts. The aims and goals for our military have shifted over the years we have covered in this book. For example, America as a nation and people were highly successful in helping to bring about peace during the two World Wars and emerged from the Second World War as the major player in the Western World. America founded NATO and helped to establish the United Nations. Unfortunately our elected officials do not see fit to support the United Nations by failing to authorize money for that purpose. We did attempt to make the Korean conflict a war conducted under the blue flag of the United Nations and did have several allies in the early days of that war although it quickly became an American war and continued as that until the end. According to our Constitution only Congress can declare war, and America has not done so since World War II, although the U. S. asked and received support for military interventions by the United Nations Security Council and has been allocated funds by Congress to conduct such military interventions. The Korean military intervention was first called a police action although the later conflict was a war by any standard and is presented that way in our history books and historical records.

It is hard to consider the Korean conflict's end a victory for the U. S., given that the original boundaries remained and America sustains a military presence in South Korea to this date. If our attempt to rule the world had ended with the Korean War, all might have been well. Yet, our foreign policy became mired in what was called a domino theory or the idea if one nation in Asia became communistic, the next one would do so as well. The outcome of that logic was that we had to stop the first domino from falling and that was the nation of Vietnam. You are probably familiar with the most significant failure of U. S. foreign policy, the Vietnam War, which was based on a mistaken theory that America must contain the spread of Communism into the Far East. When France withdrew from Indochina after its failure against the Vietnamese army in 1954, American forces replaced the French. France agreed to a meeting of nations regarding Indochina in Geneva with the result the Geneva Accords (not to be confused with the Geneva Convention) although America and its token ally South Vietnam did not sign the Accords. The result of the Accords was the partitioning of Vietnam into North Vietnam controlled by the government of Ho Chi Min in Hanoi and the southern part controlled by a quasi-government overseen by the U. S. based in Saigon. The conflict in the Southeast had a long past as the Asian nations fought to remove the colonial powers from their sphere which was delayed by World War II and this conflict re-emerged after World War II and ended with Mainland China becoming a communist nation and it was feared that other nations in that region would follow. Hence, first under Kennedy and later Johnson followed by Nixon that war formally began in 1954 and only ended with the U. S. withdrawal in 1975. There is no real way to determine the dollar cost of that war, but the human cost was great. It is estimated that at least three million Asians were killed of which fifty percent were civilians. By contrast the U. S. lost fifty-eight thousand military personnel killed.

The result of that war and its end had major ramifications for years. As the war dragged on with the continued drafting of people for the military, protests at home and abroad reached a significantly high level. Many of the U. S. war protesters were college students who had obtained deferments to attend college and were fearful that they might have to serve after graduation. Also there was a significant group of people were we opposed to war of any kind and they joined with the college students.

One may attain information regarding the world-wide military facts from the Stockholm International Peace Research Institute that publishes an annual report. For the 2013 year, American leads in money spent ($682 billion U. S. Dollars) followed by China ($166 billion USD), Russia ($91 billion USD), The United Kingdom ($61 billion USD), and Japan ($59 billion USD). The amount budgeted by the Congress for defense has climbed from roughly $300 billion in 2001 to $525 billion in 2013. This amount does not include all costs that will accrue.

A brief review of U. S. military interventions after the end of the Vietnam War include eleven such actions. At best, only three can be seen as clear wins for America. These are the raid on Libya during the Reagan administration, the invasion of Panama, and the first Gulf War. Several of these incursions are outright failures for America including Carter's attempt to free the Marine guards captured by Iran, two deployments into Beirut, Lebanon, and the use of America forces in Somalia. The outcomes of our invasion of Haiti to restore the ousted President, and the operations in Eastern Europe areas including Bosnia and Serbia are hard to evaluate with no clear outcome. The second Gulf War at first appeared successful but the occupation dragged on and finally America withdrew without a final settlement of the long standing issues among the residents of Iraq. The results for Afghanistan are not known as that intervention is still underway.

The covert war in Nicaragua during the Reagan administration was envisioned to suppress the rebels in that country as Reagan believed they were communists. The action was a failure and eventually the activity was declared to be illegal however the actual cost was never established. In the early years of the military actions in Iraq and Afghanistan, they were funded by supplemental spending bills and therefore were not part of the Federal budget. Beginning with June, 2010 that was changed and the direct costs are in the budget. However, the indirect costs like the Veterans Administrations expenses to care for the wounded service personnel, will probably grow to exceed the direct costs, are not included.

By the end of 2008 the Iraq and Afghanistan operations had a total cost of $900 billion USD. As of June 2011 the cost of these wars was approximately $3.7 trillion.

If we could feel as we did at the end of the Second World War that America had helped to bring an end to fighting and now worked to gain peace throughout the world, I would say these costs had a positive benefit. However, America is not working for peace and has served to destabilize the Middle East with a patchwork of policy that seems to change with the winds. One major outcome of the new century is that Asia is becoming so inter-related with the West as to be co-dependent that a world war is not even an option.

By examining the costs of military hardware one can see that the United States cannot continue to repeatedly upgrade its military might as it has done in the last 20 years. The pictures on the first page of this chapter show the USS CVN 76 named for Ronald Reagan. The cost of such an aircraft carrier is hard to determine as the military and Congress want to keep the numbers small. Anti-war periodicals want to make the numbers very large. The estimates of the cost of the Ronald Reagan range from a low of 9 Billion U. S. dollars to a high of 27 Billion U. S. dollars. The figure of 22 Billion seems to be a rather well documented statistic. When you add the cost of aircraft to arm the carrier and the weapons carried by the aircraft that amount would increase substantially.

The aircraft pictured are of the F-22 Raptor Air Force jet fighter-bomber that is yet to gain full acceptance by the pilots who must fly them. There were constant delays in the manufacture of the Raptor with large cost overruns. As with an aircraft carrier the actual cost of one individual Raptor is hard to pin down. An interesting bit of mathematics shows that the unit cost will be lower when the number of planes built is increased. That overlooks the cost of the total program. Estimates of the unit cost of the Raptor are somewhere between 137 Million and 678 Million U. S. dollars. If we are to add the cost of 100 more Raptors the unit cost will be lessened, but the overall cost of the program will be greatly increased

These excessive costs are a result of what Eisenhower termed the military-industrial complex. The members of this complex have extensive monetary backing and hire ex-military officers as consultants and lobbyists who have been successful in getting increased funding above and beyond what the Defense Department has asked for. The taxpayers have been forced to pay for weaponry that the military does not want. Why? The companies that provide the military equipment are very effective in gaining support of Congress through showing how the spending will help specific areas where defense industries are a substantial component of the tax base of the cities, counties, and states.

At one point in the cold war it was estimated that America and Russia were in a race to see which would bankrupt first. Russia won but America was not far behind. Since the breakup of the Soviet Union, America's defense spending has not decreased. Rather it has increased dramatically as the previous administrations undertook ventures believed to be in the interest of America's desire to rule the world.

# PART II

## OPENING THE DOOR TO FUSION

To move from the dual thinking of East and West as separate concepts which shall never meet, we must move through a transition from this kind of thinking to that where we see the East and West as joining together as suggested by the term Fusion. We will use the parallels of the Western traditions as seen through teachings from *A Course in Miracles* and its resultant plan of study called Attitudinal Healing and the teachings of the Eastern traditions as Buddhism with its many branches. To ease us through that process we will call on the early teachings of the East and West and show the similarities that existed many years ago. We will call this transition.

To begin this transition we must first step through the Doorway to Paradise as depicted in this picture to the right.

# PROLOGUE

This book began from the premise that there is a changing relationship of the geopolitical organization that placed the West in a position of dominance in the world order as depicted in the Heartland Theory. Part I was based on an evaluation of specific aspects of American life with regard to this new world order. In the next sections were will review Eastern and Western philosophies for similarity and overlap. Part II will provide a transition from Part I to Part III which is the review of the similarities and commonalities of Eastern and Western thinking as typified by Attitudinal Healing as conceived by Gerald Jampolsky and Buddhism as it is practiced by many people of the Eastern world. To set the stage for this transition, let us consider some of the ideas of modern Western thinkers.

## From Jeffery Sachs—The Next Steps

"The great role must be played by each of us, as citizens, family members, and members of our society. For several decades now, money has trumped votes; expediency has clouded the future; and we Americans have been too distracted to defend out rights. We must now redress a society dangerously out of balance. Yet as large as these problems are, they can be overcome if we face them as a unified society, acting on shared values of freedom, justice, and regard for the future."

"Let us move forward, then, with our reason and spirit. Let each of us commit first to be good to ourselves and our long-term happiness by disconnecting from TV and the media long enough each day to regain our bearings, to read more books, to ensure that we are well-informed citizens. Let us keep abreast of science and technology—on climate change, energy systems, transportation options, and disease control—so that we can support the shared public actions needed to help secure our future. Let us study the federal budget to know what's real and what is gimmickry in our politics, so that the rich and powerful don't simply walk away with the whole prize."

"As a society, let's resolve to live up to the spirit of high accomplishment, fair play, and equality of opportunity that has defined America in its best days. America will not again dominate the world economy or geopolitics as it did in the immediate aftermath of World War II. That was a special historical moment; we can be glad that economic progress throughout the world is rapidly creating a more balanced global economy and society." (Jeffery D. Sachs, *The Price of Civilization,* Pages 262-263.)

## From Jimmy Carter—Fundamentalism in Government

Regarding the policies of the George W. Bush presidency, Carter wrote:

". . . neocons' now seem to embrace aggressive and unilateral intervention in foreign affairs, especially to advance U. S. military and political influence in the Middle East."

"Some neocons now dominate the highest councils of government, seem determined to exert American dominance throughout the world, and approve of preemptive war, as an acceptable avenue to reach this imperialist goal."

"This dependence on military force to expand America's influence and other recent deviations from traditional values has dramatically reduced the attractiveness of our political, cultural, and religious offering to the world. Although most Americans are convinced of the superiority of these attributes of our Western society, it has become increasingly obvious that a heavy-handed effort to impose them on other people can be counterproductive." (Jimmy Carter, *Our Endangered Values,* Page 100.)

## From Paul Rasor, *Democracy and Empire*

"The tension between democracy and empire seems to be a permanent feature of the American condition. By the same token; religious liberals seem cursed to live with the tension between energizing hope and the temptation toward paralyzing cynicism. But cynicism is a luxury of privilege, a negative spirituality that in the end only feeds the forces of empire. We can maintain our hope, and be true to our own religious ideals, if we remember that this very dissonance, this tension that so often frustrates us, can be creative as well as destructive. It can fuel the passion to question, the courage to be prophetic, and the faith to hope." (Paul Rasor, *Democracy and Empire*, UU World, Summer 2012, Page 35.)

# Introduction

L et us first be reminded by the statement of Sachs that the status of America in the world will never be same as was experienced in the aftermath of World War II. As noted before, those of us born before WW II lived through the era when America was the dominant power of the Western World. Those born later did not experience that era and do not understand that we must move to a new recognition of our status in the world of nations. This change in our thinking requires a transition.

Bardo is a Tibetan word that literally means an intermediate or transitional state. For Buddhists this is an important concept as they teach about several transitions in the life of a person. They also think of death as only one of several bardos and we can think of it in that sense. Thus, for our transition, we are not thinking of the death of Western culture, philosophy, or religion, as those will continue in the minds of the people. We do not expect Eastern culture, philosophy, or religion to replace the Western way, or the Western way to replace the Eastern way. Instead we think of selecting among the teachings and thoughts what best fits the current situation.

In the Western world transitions are marked by doors, and we will begin from that perspective as we honor Janus who is the keeper of the doors.

# TRANSITION

How are we to move beyond the Euro-centric thinking that has dominated U. S. Culture for many years, and make a transition to an opening to the Eastern way of thinking? "In ancient Roman religion and mythology, **Janus** (Latin: *Ianus*) is the god of beginnings and transitions, hence also of gates, doors, doorways, endings and time."

A statue representing *Janus Bifrons*
in the Vatican Museums

Roman Mythology, which was active about the time of the formal beginning of the development of western culture, offers the god Janus to be the keeper of the door. In the figure above we find Janus as a two-headed god with one head looking backward to where he was coming from and the other head looking forward toward the future. The classic example in western culture is the separation of the old year from the new with the ending of December and the beginning of January. It is Janus for whom the month of January is named. However, that is only one of many transitions. Janus oversaw doorways and in Roman mythology he opened the door in time of war and closed it in time of peace. The Arch of Janus is shown below.

Arch of Janus in the Forum Boarium, framing
the Church of St. George, Velabro

# CHAPTER SEVEN

# COMING TOGETHER

In this chapter we will use the eastern tradition of Taoism as a basis for fusion. In the Yin-yang Symbol shown below, we find the complementary areas of white and black.

The notion of the Tao, or the way, is one of the oldest philosophies to emerge from ancient China and the symbol used to describe this faith is the symbol of the Yin and Yang as depicted. Taoism can be traced backward, as if by Janus' rear-looking face, to the earliest days of Asian history. The Yin or white part of the symbol is used to refer to the masculine and the black part to the feminine. The white refers to the northern side of the mountain and to the warmth of the sun, whereas the black refers to the southern side of the mountain and the relative cold for the lack of sunshine. The symbol can be used to refer to a basic aspect of knowledge where two characteristics stand in contrast as light is to dark, warmth is to cold, male is to female, and life is to death. In all of these examples the concept of one cannot be understood without the other. We are to call on this symbol to represent the potential fusion of east and west.

Yin and Yang are complementary, rather than competing forces; one cannot know light if there is no darkness. Early Taoism emerged as the antithesis to the seemingly endless period of warfare from 475-221 BCE. That seems relevant to today as we seem to be caught up in a continuing series of wars which drain our resources and our mental health. The elements of early Taoist thought included the cycle of progression of the seasons and the birth, growth and death of individuals. Taoism (in recent times often spelled Daoism) is a practice of seeking harmony and peace. There are various writings and authors referred to in the long historical development of Taoism and the modern result is very much akin to the process that Hegel described in his writing about the solution of conflicts. In this case, in Taoism, different schools of thought have emerged and over time were merged into a single system with several parallel branches. We will use the concept of Yin and Yang as our metaphor for the fusion of east and west as east does not exist without west, and west without east. But they do exist in harmony.

Benjamin Hoff wrote a small book *The Tao of Pooh* in which he offers a cute story involving the characters of Pooh and his friends as a means of explaining Taoism to the typical westerner. One of his most interesting comments for our use is the note that if you look too hard for the Tao, or the way, you will not fine the Tao. When one asked Pooh what he was, his reply was "I am just Pooh." By just being who you are is the best way to find the Tao.

# The dialectic

In western thinking and philosophy we find the notion of the dialectic to be similar in many ways to the concept of Yin and yang. The notion of using a dialectic process to promote consensus is very old and can be found in early Indian and European writings. According to Wikipedia:

"**Dialectic** . . . is a method of argument for resolving disagreement that has been central to Indian and European philosophy since antiquity.

The term first appears in western thought in the writing of early Greeks. Plato adopted this method in his dialogues. In general the sequence of developing resolution of different answers to a question is through the practice of discussing the two sides of a question until a consensus emerges. The concept of the dialectic appears in many classic discussions of the nature of knowledge. In the western world one well known example is the work by Hegel (Georg Wilhelm Friedrich Hegel, various writings including *The Phenomenology of Spirit*, 1807). Hegel was an important German philosopher who proposed a theory of historical development that included the stages in order of:

- The original development or the idea or the *thesis.*
- A later, counter development or the idea or the *antithesis.*
- A resolution of the thesis and antithesis or the *synthesis.*

While Hegel did not use these terms they do summarize his argument. Hegel labeled this three stage process with the following terms in German:

- An-sich (In itself)
- Anderssein (Out of itself)
- An-und-fur-sich (In and out of itself)

We might make a parallel set of terms to refer to a thing which will transform over time as

- What it was.
- What it is.
- What it will be.

Thus, we have Janus as he looks to the past, the Buddhist living in bardo, and Janus looking forward. That is what we are about in this book, to look back at the old American culture, recognize it is in a state of confusion, and to look forward to the synthesis of east and west

# Historical Background

## Western Thought

Two significant and somewhat parallel events start the story of western civilization. The first is the story in Genesis in the Hebrew Bible about the birth and life of Abram who was the anointed founder of the Hebrew faith. He was born about 1900 BCE in the land of Canaan. At that time Canaan was under the protection of Egypt and due to a period of famine the family of Abram moved to Egypt and it was during his period in Egypt Abram did several significant things; he changed his name to Abraham and his wife's name to Sarah. He identified his God and made this God the one and only God of the Hebrew people. Most of the story of Abraham is conjecture and the Book of Genesis is a combination of a number of stories carried through the oral tradition until written down 1500 hundred years later. As Bruce Feiler wrote in his book *Abraham:*

"But in telling the story of Abraham, the Bible is interested in much more than history. It takes elements of history, mixes them with elements of myth, and begins to mold them into a theme.

Abraham is not a settled man, or a wandering man. He's a combination, who embodies in his upbringing a message he will come to represent: the perpetual stranger in a strange land, the outsider who longs for land, the pious who finds a palliative in God for his endlessly painful life." (P. 21)

This mythical figure of Abraham is the authority for the origin of three great religions. First, he was the father of Judaism and he proclaimed that there was only one God, Yahweh or sometimes Jehovah. His notion of God was that of a human, male figure who was the personal God of the Hebrew people. This God could feel anger as well as joy, and could harm as well as spread love. This God favored the Hebrew people over all others, yet one who could punish his people if they did not obey his laws.

The second major religion was Christianity which grew out of Judaism under the teachings and writing of Saul (later Paul). The Hebrew bible was carried along with the addition of the stories of Jesus and the teachings of Paul. The third major religion was Islam where their faith is traced back to Abraham and they use much of the text of the Hebrew bible as the first parts of the Koran.

The next step in this history is the leap forward from Abraham to Moses, a stretch of some 500 years. Once again the Hebrew people were in Egypt where they had lived for many years rather like slaves. The story of Moses is well documented in the Hebrew bible with his life and later his removal of the Hebrew nation out of Egypt back to the land of Canaan. During this trip he was said to have received the laws from Yahweh which were written on stone tablets and to be taken to his people for their understanding and adoption. Biblical scholars believe this time frame of the Exodus was 1250-1230 BCE and the period Moses led the Hebrew people in the new land lasted to his death in about 1280 BCE. Even though the laws had been given to Moses by God, the written form of the early history of the Hebrews happened most likely when the Hebrews were once again captives, although this time in Babylonia. This time span was 600-400 BCE.

# The Law

Western culture had a nonreligious beginning as well as religious. This culture began much in the same location as the origin of the stories of the Hebrew Bible. In the eastern part of the Fertile Crescent the land was arable and people could settle in cities rather than continue the nomadic lifestyle, and people who are settled and have a supply of food have leisure time to develop writing and to record stories of their people. This included the development of codified sets of laws which people were to obey. One of the most well-known set of laws was the Code of Hammurabi who was the sixth king of Babylonia and ruled from 1792-1750 BCE. The code was written in stone in pictorial form called Cuneiform in the year of 1772 BCE. Hammurabi had sets of his laws placed in public view so citizens who were literate could read them and know to follow the laws or to suffer punishments. This law was very specific and dealt with issues familiar to all of us. This document was probably important in the early writings of the Hebrews and has many similarities with the Torah as it speaks to the issues of and eye for an eye and a tooth for a tooth.

The villages during this period were based on agriculture and were dependent on rain and soil. Irrigation was common and in some cases the saline level in soil became a barrier to farming causing families to move to different areas. Out of this Fertile Crescent arouse a well advanced culture beginning with ancient Greece flourishing from 2000 to 1200 BCE when the Minoan and Mycenaean cultures were overrun by foreign armies followed by a period of dark ages which lasted until 800 BCE. Next Alexander, the Great, conquered Greece and ruled until the Romans replaced him to rule from 200 BCE until 476 CE.

## Grecian Period

The next step in this story moves to ancient Greece where Plato was born. The figure of Socrates is far from clear although some historians believe he was a fictitious creation of Plato with whom to dialog in his musing about the nature of the world. It is interesting that historical references do present him as a factual figure. From Wikipedia, we find the following quote. "Socrates, 496-399 BCE" . . . was a classical Greek Athenian philosopher. Credited as one of the founders of Western philosophy, he is an enigmatic figure known chiefly through the accounts of later classical writers, especially the writings of his students Plato and Xenophon."

A second enticing quote is "Plato never speaks in his own voice in his dialogues. In the *Second Letter,* it says 'no writing of Plato exists or ever will exist, but those now said to be his are those of a Socrates become beautiful and new.'" We are left not knowing whether Plato speaks for a mythological Socrates, or whether Plato only apes what Socrates speaks, or actually disguises his own thoughts as if they were the thoughts of the unknowable Socrates. The story of the death of Socrates may be apocryphal and was an easy way to remove Socrates from the story. In any event, a major figure in this development of western philosophy was Plato who began the codification of the history of western civilization. It is important to have a sense of the area in which Plato lived. Refer to the map of the Roman Empire (P. 7) to find that the area included was relatively small in comparison with the remaining parts of the world. Plato was born around 424 BCE. His family was well-to-do and he was able to travel to Italy, Sicily, Egypt and Cyrene. Upon his return to Athens he established the first academy for the teaching of the advanced study of Western thought. His Academy continued for several years after Plato died at the age of seventy-five but was destroyed in 84 BCE.

The basic themes of Plato's teachings were:

- That knowledge was a matter of recollection of experience rather than the result of one's direct observation of the events.
- That knowledge is gained through insight rather than by direct experience.

These notions are valid today as we try to understand why witnesses to events report vastly different experiences of the event. As Plato believed, the witnesses are stating their recollections of the event, not their direct experience of the event. Also, one may be able to describe an event thoroughly but not be able to explain the event to another person as he lacks the insight into the event.

Like Plato Aristotle was born into a well-to-do family in the year 384 BCE which would have been forty years after Plato was born. His story began when he attended Plato's Academy for 20 years during which he learned a great deal and wrote a number of dialogues much as Plato had done. Upon the death of Plato, Aristotle traveled and studied natural events. Later he returned to Athens and opened his own school in 334 BCE known as the Lyceum. It is believed that much of his work has been lost although he profoundly affected the Christian and Muslin scholars. Thomas Aquinas wrote that he believed Aristotle knew more about the world than any other philosopher. Aristotle's teachings were carried forward up to the time that Rene Descartes initiated what was termed the modern era of philosophy.

Aristotle worked with logic and reasoning and is well known for his use of syllogisms such as the following.

- All sheep are animals.
- We own a sheep.
- Therefore, our sheep must be an animal.

Also

- All human beings have DNA.
- My son is a human being.
- Therefore, he must have DNA.

**Souls**

Aristotle thought of the human being as having three souls. These souls he named as:

Nutritive.                     Sensory.                     Thinking.

There is a striking parallel with the idea much later proposed by Sigmund Freud when he divided the self into three components. Freud named his parts as the Id, Ego, and Superego, where the Id represents the basic biological urges for survival, the Ego represents the aware and active human being, and the Superego is much like our notion of conscience where we use reason to evaluate what we do.

Another interesting case is the one of the elements of the world. Aristotle believed that we could understand and describe our world in terms of fire, water, air, and earth. Yet he added one more element,

Aether, which was the ". . . divine substance that makes up the heavenly spheres and bodies of the universe." Later scientists would postulate that ether was the means whereby light was transmitted through space as space was nearly a vacuum and sound could not travel in a vacuum. Thus there must be some element whereby light could travel in a vacuum. Because light could not travel in a vacuum, a substance was needed to allow for the travel of light and this substance was called ether. Only later did we understand that light was very different from sound and did not need a medium for it to travel through space. But we still find the concept of ether to hang on even into the computer age with ether nets.

## SUMMARY

We have a long history of the people that constituted the western world, most of which we find in the Hebrew Bible which served as the basis for the Christian Bible and the Muslin Koran. When Greece was at its height we found three philosophers, Socrates, Plato, and Aristotle who brought together the knowledge of the time along philosophical lines not tied to religion. Yet their work was that which truly established a specific set of knowledge and beliefs that under lay the future development of western civilization. The strong scientific element to Western culture was begun with Aristotle and has continued to this day.

# The Origins of Eastern
# Philosophy and Religion

To set a context in terms of the relative size of the major religions; we will find that Christianity is the largest with about thirty-three percent of the total. Islam is second with twenty percent of the total and Hinduism with thirteen percent and Buddhism with six percent. The smaller religions account for thirteen percent while nonreligious people make up fifteen percent. Judaism accounts for only 0.2 percent of the total.

## Hinduism

In the very early days of India, (5500-2600 BCE), there was some evidence of religious practices which evolved into modern day Hinduism. The more recent history (1500-500 BCE) was called the period of Vedic religion when the Veda, the oldest scripture of Hinduism, was composed dated 1700-1100 BCE. Later during the 9th and 8th centuries BCE a set of documents called the Upanishads were composed to form the theoretical basis for Hinduism. As would be expected, there was a continuing evolution of the Hindu faith with the addition of epics of various sources. In the early centuries, CE, the several differing schools of Hindu thought and practice were codified into several sets of texts.

Near the 6th Century CE Arab traders began to travel into the western parts of India and they brought Islam with them and that impact is still present today as when the British left India the outcome was the formation of Pakistan as a Muslin Country while India remained predominately Hindu. Hinduism continues to be a major religious force in Asia and is the third largest religion in the world following Christianity and Islam. There are numerous schools of thought with some differences not unlike the many Christian variations throughout the world.

## Buddhism

Buddhism is named for the original teacher of what was to become a major form of religious and philosophical thinking in Asia. The historical Buddha was born into a wealthy family and had the title of Prince. Historians do not have a specific date of his birth, but believe he lived sometime during the fifth and sixth centuries, BCE. His name was Siddhartha Gautama and he resided in the area between India and Nepal. He lived in luxury but with the typical curiosity of a young man, he left the palace and went among the common people where he found poverty and sickness. This troubled him to the extent that he left his home and luxurious living to meditate and later to teach or preach. There are many parallels with the life of Jesus and that of Gautama. Once a person encountered the man now called Buddha and asked if he was enlightened. The Buddha answered that he "Was awake." The beginning of Buddhism was based on the teachings of the Buddha taught orally and later by written copies of his teachings. At some point the tradition of a Lama or teacher was developed and these persons traveled widely teaching their understanding of Buddhism. They were often poor and actually begged for food and lodging.

Later a supreme Lama, the Dalai Lama, was developed in which a young man determined by the elders was selected in the early teens for special teachings; he later assumed the role of the Dalai Lama. A major geographical area of Buddhist teaching was developed in Tibet but when the Chinese took over Tibet the Lama was forced to flee for his life and now resides in India near the northern border. According to one source, there are 10,000 Buddhist temples in Hong Kong which offers a sense of the size and importance of this faith.

Thubten Chodron in his book *Buddhism for Beginners* (2001) wrote about the essence of Buddhism: "Simply speaking, it is to avoid harming others and to help them as much as possible." Another way of expressing this is the oft-quoted verse:

> Abandon negative action;
> Create perfect virtue;
> Subdue your own mind.
> This is the teaching of the Buddha.

Buddhism offers the concept of the path or the way which is also prominent in Taoism. In short we can say that we are here on earth to seek the way which will lead us to attain Nirvana. But, both the way and Nirvana are left undefined as only you can know them.

## Taoism

Taoism is a philosophy or religion that emphasizes the Tao or the way; the Tao is the pathway to achievement of wholeness and peace. Laozi is believed to have lived in the 6th century BCE although some believe he lived later. He preceded Confucius by several years and there are stories that the two met although that cannot be verified. As mentioned earlier, Taoism was developed as the antithesis to the prolonged period of war around 450 BCE. Taoism sought to introduce the practice of non-action, detachment, the strength of softness and the search for a long life. The major work of Taoism is the Tao Te Ching, of which there are several sources.

For this chapter the reference is from the *Mystical Classics of the World*, Tao Te Ching, *The Classic Book of Integrity and the Way* by Lao Tzu. The following quotations offer an insight into the thinking behind the Tao.

> "The supreme perfection of actionlessness
> He attains through renunciation."
> "While you . . .
> Focus your breath until it is supremely soft,
> Can you be like a baby?"
> "What is the use of running when we are not on the right way?

As for most eastern religions their origins are traced back to a time when there were many gods and the teachings involved shamanism and pantheism, with a major focus on the cycles of life as with the seasons and the life of human beings. The many religions of Asia gained and lost support with changes in the major leaders of the era, and of course they were suppressed during the early communist regimes.

## Where is god (God) in these religions?

Western philosophy has many original sources; western religion, including Judaism, Christianity, and Islam, trace their origins to Abraham and to his personal God known by several names such as Yahweh and Allah as well as the generic name God used by Christians. Even though Muhammad was born roughly five hundred years after Jesus, he traced Allah back to the teachings and testing by the God of Abraham. By contrast eastern philosophies akin to western religions do not have the concept of a single, universal God, or god. From Wikipedia, *Oriental_religion*, "Much like the classical Greek philosophies, many Eastern schools of thought were more interested in explaining the natural world via universal patterns; without recourse to capricious agencies like gods (or God)." Many westerns argue that eastern philosophies do not have a God and therefore are not truly a religion. Certainly in eastern thinking persons do not submit to a god as did Abraham following the many tests of his faith by God. One need not become distracted by what seems to be a subtle distinction that is not made by most persons whether of western or eastern origin. Thich Nhat Hanh sees the parallels of Christian and Buddhist teaching and presents his views in a book *Living Buddha, Living Christ*. Once he was asked by a Catholic priest to tell him about Buddhism. Hahn asked the priest to "share his understanding of the Holy Spirit." The priest answered that the Holy Spirit is the energy sent by God. Hahn liked that comment as he too believes that the Holy Spirit manifests God. At one point the Pope expressed the notion that Jesus was different from men like Socrates, Buddha, and Mohammed. The Pope wrote that "Jesus is absolutely original and absolutely unique." Hahn commented that this statement does not seem to reflect the Trinity. Of course, Christ is unique, but so are we all. Hahn commented that the idea behind the Pope's statement ". . . is the notion that Christianity provides the only way to salvation and all other religious traditions are of no use." He continued to comment that this attitude excludes dialogue and fosters religious intolerance.

If we are willing to accept the Easterner's sense of the Holy Spirit as akin to the Western idea of God and energy that God breathes into the followers of the faith, then we can accept that the Eastern philosophies are religions in the same sense that Western philosophies are religions.

## A note on calendars

One major contrast between the east and west is its calendar. Westerners allowed the power of Rome to dictate the western calendar and used the presumed birth year of Jesus as the starting point of the modern era. However there are other legitimate calendars for the west as the Hebrew calendar which begins with the estimated moment of creation of the earth which is 3,760 years before the birth of Jesus. The Islamic calendar begins with the flight of Muhammad' from Mecca to Medina. For the East, the Chinese calendar was important to establish the dates of events such as the seasons and lunar cycles and use of calendars can be traced backward to the 14th century, BCE. However, the zero date was set by the emperor in power around 2700 BCE and corresponds to the western year of 2,637 BCE. My point here is to emphasize that calendar dates are arbitrary and no one is better than any other. We might just as well have taken a date for the start of the Roman calendar as 1772 when Hammurabi's code was first written, or any other significant date. In any event, having different calendars does make comparison of different cultures difficult.

# PART III
## EAST AND WEST IN FUSION

*M*ay *all beings enjoy happiness and the root of happiness, May they be free from suffering and the root of suffering, May they not be separated from the great happiness devoid of suffering, May they dwell in the great equanimity free from passion, aggression and prejudice.*

Traditional Buddhist prayer

*PARALLELS OF ATTITUDINAL HEALING AND BUDDHISM*

# INTRODUCTION

P ART III explores the similarities of the East and West with an eye toward finding similarities in the two systems of thought that could be merged in what I have termed fusion. PART I reviewed aspects of Western culture for weaknesses that could be moderated by introducing aspects of eastern philosophy into western culture. The century old heartland theory focused America's foreign policy on Europe and especially the eastern parts of Europe as a means of enforcing its will on the world as a whole. This theory has been offered as a basis for western culture to dominate the world through control of the crucial area of Eastern Europe termed the pivot. This plan implies that the Western nations are to control the world as Western culture is superior to all others. History appears to have supported that belief up to the mid twentieth century with European nations establishing colonies throughout the world and with Britain maintaining that the sun never set on the British Empire. That phase of world dominance ended with World Wars I and II although America emerged as the major power of the Western world. Following WW II America was the leader of the western world and had the sole possession of the Atomic bomb. Its peak in world standing was in 1945 and America's attempt to make the world its empire has come to a halt with failures of military actions in the Far East and Middle East. Several additional changes have affected the status of America in the world order such as the breakup of the Soviet Union; so long as the Soviet Union and the United States were balanced one against the other, the world was roughly divided into two spheres of roughly equal size and power. Following the loss of this balance of power, the rise in the Asian nations' economic wealth and globalization of the economy, a new world order is emerging which clearly will make the Heartland theory obsolete. In this new world order we envision that America will play the role of one nation among many rather than one nation above all.

If and when the East and West can respect each other and share their knowledge, a genuine period of peace could result. Co-jointly we can establish a sense of balance in the world to enhance the quality of life for the individual and bring a more balanced sense to our economic practices among nations. Jeffery Sachs has done a very important thing by showing how we can gain by applying the idea of mindfulness as practiced in many Eastern traditions to Western culture. There are numerous aspects of American life that could benefit by adopting a mindful approach; to be mindful is to be aware of what we are doing to our world and to others when we take actions. In Buddhist terms, we need to use Right Thought as we go about our lives. When we sit in a drive-up lane at a McDonald's with our car's engine running, we are not being mindful of the effect that has on the environment and the world as we burn fossil fuels with little regard to its impact on the world. The mindful one will park his or her car, shut off the engine, and walk into the store.

A related issue has to do with physical and mental health in the West. Within the last fifty years Western practitioners have become increasingly aware of the inter-relation of mind and body and have looked to Eastern practices for answers to some pressing issues in health in the U. S. Referring to the negative areas in which America leads the world, we find a poor sense of peace and security, excessive crime rates, and use of legal and illegal drugs. One major author, Caroline Myss, has included much from Eastern teachings into her work as a medical intuitive. In her book *Why People Don't Heal and How They Can* she introduces the reader to the idea from Eastern medicine concerning what are called Chakras. The chakras refer to the traditional seven energy centers of the body which are believed to be the inter-connection of body to spirit. By attending to these aspects of our body, we can enhance spiritual and physical wellbeing.

Caroline Myss wrote:

> "Knowledge of the chakras has existed for thousands of years, although only in the last century has it filtered through to the West in any great detail. According to the Hindu and Buddhist metaphysical systems, the seven Chakras are the traditional energy centers of the astral body, a subtle energy plane that coexists with the physical body."

In a later chapter she noted that this view of the body is actually quite ancient.

> "The teachings and the scriptures from the Buddhist, Hindu, Hebrew, and Christian spiritual traditions all make reference to the seven sacred levels of power that contain and manage the life-force that flows through the body. The symbolism of the seven Chakras, the Tree of Life of the Jewish Kabbalah, and the seven Christian sacraments represents an internal road map, a spiritual maturation process that can lead us from the unconscious to the conscious mind, then on to the super conscious."

Caroline Myss has demonstrated how to share the wisdom of the East and the West in a meaningful manner for the value of all peoples. The blending of East and West can provide an approach to a sustainable world where we Westerners are mindful of how we think, feel, and act. Similarly the Easterners can adopt some of the technology of the West to be incorporated into the practices of the East. A recent work by His Holiness, the Fourteenth Dalai Lama, Tenzin Gyatso, supports this aim. He wrote in his book, *The Universe In A Single Atom* (2005), that the goals for this book are:

> "... I believe that spirituality and science are different but complementary investigative approaches with the same greater goal, of seeking the truth. In this, there is much we can learn from the other, and together they may contribute to expanding the horizon of human knowledge and wisdom." (Page 4)

> "Regardless of different personal views about science, no credible understanding of the natural world or our human existence—what I am going to call in this book a worldview—can ignore the basic insights of theories as key as evolution, relativity, and quantum mechanics." (Page 5)

With these two very compelling quotes by His Holiness, we will end this brief introduction to our presentation of the parallels of Eastern and Western thinking. I consider the Dalai Lama's view of science rests with what we call Western thought while spirituality rests with Eastern thought. May we come to a general inter-mixing of East and West, Science and Spirituality, a long awaited fusion . . . ?

# Background for Eastern and Western Philosophy and Religion

## Eastern traditions

The modern traditions of eastern philosophy and religion developed from ancient traditions with many gods having different roles in the scheme of things. Included are practices we might call pagan and pantheistic, although not unlike those of western practices up to the tenth century CE. Generally the modern versions do not conflict any more than the competing schools of thought in western religions. Buddhism offers an archetypal example for this work even though it is one among several of the major eastern religions. Typical Buddhism grew out of an oral tradition which was passed from generation to generation. Only later were these teachings recorded in documents to form a scripture. However, one of the important aspects of eastern religions is that they do not rely on scripture as the source of the teachings and scripture is not taken as dogmatic truth. The most crucial element of these religions is the practice of it by followers. Herein lays a major contrast in Eastern and Western thinking. Western religions stem from the Hebrew Scriptures with their heavy reliance on strict laws as those of the Code of Hammurabi and the laws of Moses and the strict regulation of the Jewish people in the Hebrew Bible. The Eastern thinking is that one must discover the way to enlightenment through personal experience and the practice of the teachings of the earlier enlightened ones. Only through practice will one discover the path to fulfillment. The individual may select those practices to follow unlike the Western people who must obey all the laws. A related issue is that in western religions records are well maintained and numbers of adherents are fairly accurate. For eastern religions this is not true so comparisons of numbers between eastern and western religious groupings are not meaningful.

The story of the founding of Buddhism is traced to a 6th century BCE mystic who adopted the name Buddha which in Sanskrit means the awakened one. The Buddha was a young man named Siddhartha Gautama who was born to a royal family and lived in luxury. He was expected to follow his father as the emperor of the region. As common for many young men, he rebelled and traveled outside of the royal compound. He was quite surprised to see that there was poverty and suffering among the citizens of his city. This puzzled him greatly and he undertook a pilgrimage to seek answers to his many questions. He lived in the north eastern part of ancient India and was reported to have spent many hours sitting beneath a tree seeking enlightenment. However, when he was approached and asked if he were enlightened, he answered only that he "Was Awake." His main discovery was that suffering was a normal part of life and could be endured in order to find peace. Thubten Chodron wrote the following:

## "Must we be a Buddhist to practice what the Buddha taught?"

"No. The Buddha gave a wide variety of instructions, and if some of them help us live better, to solve our problems, and become kinder, then we are free to practice them. There is no need to call ourselves Buddhists. The purpose of the Buddha's teachings is to benefit us, and if putting some of them into practice helps us live more peacefully with ourselves and others, that is what's important." (Page 17)

The heart of the teachings of the Buddha is The Four Noble Truths regarding *dukkha* which means suffering, anxiety, and dissatisfaction. These truths then are:

- The truth of suffering.
- The truth of the origin of suffering.
- The truth of the cessation of suffering.
- The truth of the path leading to the cessation of suffering.

Alongside of these four noble truths Buddha also suggested the means to reach an enlightened state of awareness by his eightfold factor for the awakened life. These all involve what Buddha deemed to be the best or right vantages. These involve daily activities that affect our life and our interactions with others. They are:

- Right view
- Right intention
- Right speech
- Right action
- Right livelihood
- Right effort
- Right mindfulness
- Right concentration

For Right View, the modifier is to view reality as it is rather than how it appears to be. If that sounds vague it is. You will find a similar notion in *Attitudinal Healing* and in *A Course in Miracles*. We often accept a view of reality without looking more deeply into that reality, and the Buddha asks that we recognize that we often create a reality that is faulty. In all these examples, we are asked to slow down and be mindful of what we are doing. Also, it is important that we anticipate the consequences of our views, speech, and action before we move ahead. By using meditation to help us focus, by being mindful in our actions, and by seeking the middle path, we are well along the way to nirvana. We will recognize that all things are interconnected in that each of us is influenced by others as we influence them. In short, there are many aspects of Buddhism that are stressed in some branches more than in others, although generally the branches are compatible and not in conflict. We are not here to make a Buddhist of the reader, but to prepare the reader for the later work where we will highlight the similar teachings of the eastern and western way of thinking as typified by Buddhism from the eastern perspective and *A Course in Miracles* (*The Course*) and *Attitudinal Healing* as developed by Gerald Jampolsky from *The Course*.

Perhaps the best way to present the Buddhist perspective is through the idea of Sangha-building which is considered to be the most important work the Masters do.

> Buddha is the teacher showing the way,
> the perfectly awakened one,
> beautifully seated, peaceful; and smiling,
> the living source of understanding and compassion.

This continues:

> Dharma is the clear path
> leading us out of ignorance
> bringing us back
> to an awakened life.
>
> Sangha is the beautiful community
> that practice joy,
> realizing liberation,
> bringing peace and happiness to life.

The ideal toward which the Master strives is one of building Sangha, or the perfect community, much as you would see at Plum Village outside of Paris, France, where Thich Nhat Hanh spends part of each year of his life.

## References for this section

There are many sources for information on Buddhism, and I cannot list them all. But I will list the major sources I have used in this chapter.

- Thubten Chodron. *Buddhism for Beginners*. Snow Lion Publications, New York. 2001.
- Steve Hagen. Buddhism *plain and simple*. Charles E. Tuttle Co, Inc. Boston. 1997.

- Thich Nhat Hanh. *Living Buddha, Living Christ.* Riverhead Books, New York. 1995.
- Thich Nhat Hanh. *The Heart of the Buddha's Teaching.*
- Broadway Books, New York. 1998.
- Sogyal Rinpoche. *The Tibetan Book of Living and Dying.*
- HarperSanFranciso, San Francisco. 1993.
- Saki Santorelli. *Heal Thy Self.* Lessons on Mindfulness in Medicine. Bell Tower, New York. 1999.
- Lama Surya Das. *Buddha is as Buddha Does.* Harper One. New York, 2007.
- Lao Tzu. *Tao Te Ching.* Quality Paperback Book Club, New York, 1990.

## The Western traditions

Rather than the parallel development of several eastern traditions, the western tradition is linear in that we must begin with Abraham and continue through the Hebrew Bible which is adopted and adapted by Christianity and Islam. Islam does not fit into this paradigm easily and tends to present itself as antagonistic to Christianity and eastern religions such as Hinduism. As mentioned earlier Arab traders began to travel into Eastern India for economic reasons and they carried their beliefs with them which set up an eventual conflict between the Muslims and Hindus in India. When England left India the conflict heightened to the extent that India was separated into a Muslim country of Pakistan and a Hindu country of India.

With minor exceptions modern western religions are an evolution of the early Hebrew teachings as presented in the Hebrew Bible with the addition of a new testament which introduces Jesus and his teachings into Christianity. *A Course in Miracles* presents a very clear and strong Christian message in which Jesus is presented much as the early church defined in the terms of father, son and the holy spirit. *The Course* offers an updated version of the Christian Bible and teaches the lessons through the Workbook for Students and the Manual for Teachers which are published as part of the latest version of The Course. The full reference is *A Course In Miracles, Combined Volume*, 2nd Edition, published by the Foundation for Inner Peace, 1996.

Gerald Jampolsky is a physician and a trained psychiatrist who was born into a Jewish family and was practicing medicine in California where he first encountered *The Course.* He was a faculty member of the Medical School of the University of California in San Francisco and was staff psychiatrist at a hospital in Tiburon, California. For him this was a period of stress, as he had everything one would expect in publications, presentation, status, salary, etc. But he was going through a bad time involving a divorce, a problem with this use of alcohol, and a feeling that he was stagnating. It was a synchronicity when *The Course* was handed to him and he realized how it could help him. He was working with young children with life threatening diseases and believed that more was needed than medical treatment, especially in the spiritual realm. He had noticed that the well family members needed support as so much of the energy went to the ill child. He started support groups for the families of children in the hospital as he found that the family was deeply affected by the illness of their child. From this beginning he developed the Center for Attitudinal Healing based on the notion that "love is letting go of fear." He next took the statement from *The Course* about teaching only love as the foundation for his book *Teach Only Love* in which he laid out his notion of principals for what he termed attitudinal healing. He believed that much of human suffering was the result of how a person viewed the situation and that if one would work to change how he or she viewed the situation, things would be better. The result from this experience was the establishment of the Center for Attitudinal Healing in northern California in 1975 and with the publication of his first book, *Teach Only Love,* in 1983. His book became a best seller and he later published a new-expanded edition in 2000.

His central question was must we travel through life feeling unloved and alone, afraid of sickness and death, afraid of God, and even afraid of continuing to live? He thought there must be a better way. That thinking led to several questions of which the first two were:

- Is there another way of looking at the world that changes our experience of life?
- Is it possible to choose to let go of fear and conflict completely?

He summarized his thinking with the idea that most of our issues in life are not caused by other persons or events in the world, but our interpretation of these events. And, if that is so, then we can work to change our reaction to these events, and thereby change how we feel about them. From his work he developed a listing of twelve principles on which he based his program of Attitudinal Healing

The twelve principles of Attitudinal Healing:

1. The essence of our being is love.
2. Health is inner peace.
3. Giving and receiving are the same.
4. We can let go of the past and the future.

5. Now is the only time there is.
6. We can learn to love ourselves and others by forgiving rather than judging.
7. We can become love-finders rather the faultfinders.
8. We can be peaceful inside regardless of what is happening outside.
9. We are students and teachers to each other.
10. We can focus on the whole of our lives rather than on the fragments.
11. Because love is eternal, death need not be viewed as fearful.
12. We can always see ourselves and others as extending love or giving a call for help.

In a brief summary Jampolsky came to understand that he could change how he felt about specific events by changing his attitude. While this is not a new or unique idea, it is common to find that all people must come to this conclusion on their own. William James reached a similar conclusion as he was moving through a period of depression and had read a French philosopher who wrote that all we needed to have freewill was to believe we had it. In the development of Cognitive Behavior therapy by Aaron Beck, we find the basic idea is that we can change how we feel by changing our actions and our thoughts. Cognitive behavior therapy is the most widely accepted psychological intervention for depression.

> Jampolsky wrote as follows: "The mind can be retrained. Within this fact lies our freedom. No matter how often we have misused it, the mind can be utilized in a way that is so positive that at first it is beyond anything we can imagine." (*Teach Only Love*).

These are not new ideas, and, as is common with enlightenment each person must come to understand this process by its practice. That is a key point in both Attitudinal Healing and Buddhism in that it is not knowing these points but to put them to use in your daily life.

In the next chapters we will examine the similarities of Buddhism and its teaching about love with those offered by *The Course* and *Attitudinal Healing.*

# CHAPTER EIGHT

# WE ARE LOVE

## THE FIRST PRINCIPLE OF
## ATTITUDINAL HEALING

J ampolsky understands that this principle is almost a summary of the entire concept of *Attitudinal Healing*. You will find that love appears often in all major philosophies of life in all cultures.

Jampolsky explains this principle in this way:

*"The essence of our being is love.* Love cannot be hindered by what is merely physical. Therefore, we believe the mind has no limits; nothing is impossible; and all disease is potentially reversible. And because love is eternal, death need not be viewed fearfully."

To begin let's ask the question of how does Buddhism relates to this first principle of Attitudinal Healing? Love is a fundamental element of the teachings found in the *Hebrew Bible*, the *Christian Bible*, *A Course in Miracles*, and *Attitudinal Healing*. The original law given to Moses asks that you love your neighbor as yourself. As all are interconnected, your neighbor is all other people and you are to love them all. Jesus repeats this teaching in his many sermons to his followers. It is a short jump to *The Course* (Chapter 6, THE LESSONS OF LOVE, III-2):

"This is why you must teach only one lesson. If you are to be conflict-free yourself, you must learn only from the Holy Spirit and teach only by Him. You are only love, but when you deny this, you make what you are something you must learn to remember."

"Teach only love, for that is what you are."

"This is the one lesson that is perfectly unified, because it is the only lesson that is one."

"Only by teaching it can you learn it. If this is true, and it is true indeed, do not forget that what you teach is teaching you."

Jampolsky shared an interesting incident in his book *Teaching Only Love* that relates to using love to counter fear. Jampolsky and his wife had traveled to Peru to do a workshop on Attitudinal Healing. They had some free time and went for a hike seeking a Shaman. They did encounter a Shaman who was the healer for a small village. Jampolsky, through a translator, asked the Shaman how he dealt with mental illness. The Shaman answered that we give him or her love. The Shaman suggested that the illness was the result of fear, and love will counter that fear. That idea is very closely related to the teachings of *The Course* and in Attitudinal Healing. Jampolsky asked about individuals who become hurtful and destructive, the Shaman simply replied that we just give him more love. That would be the way of the Bodhisattva.

Integration of the teachings of the Buddha is found in modern psychotherapy methods. One example is the treatment tactic called Dialectical Behavior Therapy developed by Marsha M. Linehan in her work with borderline personality disorders. In this model the patient is asked to apply the process of dialectic problem solving coupled with mindfulness training and meditation. In a parallel development Jon Kabat-Zinn has been teaching meditation and mindfulness to his clients in his stress reduction program. These are examples of how

Buddhist thinking has come into modern American Psychology and Psychiatry, demonstrating a strong link between eastern and western spiritual practices. As these practices come into medicine, they may begin to enter into other fields such as economics as Sachs mentioned in his writings.

## THE BUDDHA'S TEACHING ABOUT LOVE

People of the Brahmanic faith believed upon their death they would go to be with the Brahma in heaven. They asked the Buddha how to ensure that they would be among the chosen few. The Buddha answered: "As the Brahma is the source of Love, to dwell with him you must practice the 'Brahma Abodes,' . . . or Four Immeasurable Minds—love, compassion, joy, and equanimity." He continued by saying that love, compassion, joy, and equanimity are the very nature of the enlightened one. They are the four aspects of true love within ourselves and everyone and everything. We all have the seeds of love within us and we can develop this source of energy which brings forth unconditional love while expecting nothing in return.

Much of Eastern philosophy and religion is about love such that the topic is rarely addressed directly. It is more or less assumed that the enlightened one extrudes love all the while he or she is teaching others about the way. From the writings of Lama Surya Das we encounter his book *Buddha Is As Buddha Does* (2007). The title makes an important point that one may learn about Buddhism but unless one practices the way one is not truly enlightened. I tell my students to watch what therapists do rather then what they say they do. If you want to learn how to be enlightened, you must practice the way. Das wrote in the Preface that this book is a map to the richest treasure a human being may have. Furthermore, if you follow its guidelines you will enter into a new way of life. That is the essence of Buddhism. Love simply comes along with the practice.

This path is called the Bodhisattva Code and the ones who follow it become Bodhisattvas. The practice need not be labeled as it is not a theory or an ism; it is a code one must follow. Regarding love, Das wrote "The minute you start reading these pages you can begin to reorient your life in the bold, exciting, and inspiring Bodhisattva direction of truth and love." When asked how to respond to the troubling times of today, Tibetan master Khenpo Thrangu Rinpoche replied:

> "You must counter the negative energy with as much positive thought and action as you can possible muster. You must unceasingly sustain Bodhisattva action. It is the Buddha's teaching to make ourselves an example, a light, a beacon." (Das, Page XXI.)

Note the similar language in this statement about using the practice to counter the negative thoughts to what is written in *The Course* about love countering fear and *Attitudinal Healing* where we recognize that love is the absence of fear. For the enlightened one the practice is filled with our expressions of love.

For the Buddha true love must contain compassion joy, and equanimity. When the Buddha told the Brahman man to practice the Four Immeasurable Minds, he was also offering all of us a very important teaching. We must practice the four aspects of truth to bring love into our minds and the minds of others.

# CHAPTER NINE

# OUR GOAL IS PEACE

## THE SECOND PRINCIPLE OF ATTITUDINAL HEALING:

> The principle is: "*Health is inner peace. Healing is letting go of fear.* To make changing the body our goal is to fail to recognize that our single goal is peace of mind."

From this principle we find the terms of peace, fear, and healing appearing and they will appear again and again in the study of *Attitudinal Healing*. We also will find these same concepts in the teachings of the Eastern masters. For example, Jampolsky wrote:

> "There often appears to be a philosophical and spiritual joining of East and West within these teachings. Most of these systems teach that the thoughts we hold determine our experience and then explain how we can change our perceptions of ourselves and the world. Attitudinal Healing has a similar objective, because once we begin to remove the barriers to our perception of love's presence, we can begin to heal ourselves on every level and in every way."

I would interpret the phrase "Most of these systems . . . ." to refer to those of the East. I do see the parallel of Eastern teachings with those of Attitudinal Healing. The main Western religion that teaches about healing is Christian Science, although most religions do train Chaplains who work with the ill and dying members of their faiths. Most professionals who work with people who are experiencing stress will suggest meditation, long walks, exercise, yoga, and similar activities that will ease the signs of stress. One point that the early writer about stress, Hans Selye (*The Stress of Life,* 1956), made was that stress occurs due to the person's reaction to events rather than the event itself. Some people react to heights very strongly and avoid them while others are not bothered by heights. Therefore professionals working with clients judge the individual's reaction to events in planning programs for relief.

Jampolsky ended this chapter with the following:

"To be free of fear requires only one thing: A goal that is itself not fearful."

"Make this instant your door to freedom and you will find that it will crack open a little further each time you return to this moment in peace."

## THE BUDDHIST'S PERSPECTIVE ON THE GOAL OF LIFE TO BE PEACE

While western writers may not use the same words as the eastern writers, we are speaking about the same things. Just as Jampolsky believes that we are seeking inner peace, the Buddha and other enlightened ones, teach practices to bring us inner peace and healing.

In many of the stories of western writers we find the common theme of the fall and recovery (Calhoun, *The Fall and Beyond*, 2008). While living a typical life of the western person, people may have a serious fall that stops them in their tracks and they must adjust their lives to recover from and resist another fall. We can find a similar path for the Buddha who had his major shock when he traveled outside of the palace to find that people were poor, ill and suffering. These observations started him on his path to peace and harmony. Thereby he began his teaching with the Four Noble Truths. The first truth is that we all suffer. We often have four questions we want someone to answer. These are:

- Where did I come from?
- Why am I here?
- Where will I go?
- What do I do in the meantime?

These are universal questions and all known religions and philosophies strive to offer answers to these questions. Such questions and suggested answers are not bound by national boundaries, languages spoken, or belief systems of the culture.

From Buddhism we learn of the four Noble Truths which speak to us of the suffering in the world. When the Buddha first left his sheltered home in the palace he encountered suffering. This is the beginning of his understanding of suffering and his realization that suffering was the basis of most human dissatisfaction. Thus the First Noble Truth was to recognize that suffering is universal and we all suffer at sometimes and others for all times. Once we have accepted our suffering, we must look into our suffering very deeply until we can see the source of our suffering. The Second Noble Truth is about the origin or cause of our suffering. Only if we look deeply into our experience of suffering can we come to understand why we suffer. The Third Noble Truth is that once we have come to understand the source of our suffering, we must learn how to avoid the continuation of our suffering. For one, we must forgo wanting more and striving for more. We have what we need at this time and place. An example of suffering from western capitalism is the belief that we do not have enough and we must therefore continue to amass more. This is an external force of wanting that will drive one to desperation and unwise action. If we can only look at this from the point of view that we really do have enough and we do not need to strive for more and ever more. The final or Fourth Noble Truth is the one that puts us on the journey to living the Noble Enlightened pathway to peace. Meditation is the key to reaching the Fourth Noble Truth. Meditation should offer you at least two things—looking deeply into your soul, and, taking time to stop all the distractions of your mind.

There is an interesting story mentioned by Thich Nhat Hanh in *The Heart of Buddha's Teaching.* Here is a story in Zen circles about a man and a horse. The horse is galloping quickly, and it appears that the man on the horse is going somewhere important. Another man, standing alongside the road, shouts, 'Where are you going?' and the first man replies, "I don't know! Ask the horse." (Page 24.)

He wrote that the man on the horse was a metaphor for our lives as we are riding a horse although we do not know where we are going or why we are going. To stop is to bring the horse a halt, get down, and take some time to look deeply into what we are doing. That is the purpose of stopping. Some time ago I spoke to a well-known therapist about stopping. I said that I thought everyone around the age of forty-five years should stop, turn around, and look from whence he or she had come. My friend stated that "Most persons do have the courage to do that." The Buddha tells us to take that as a challenge to stop and look deeply. When we meditate we do four things: meditation tells us to stop ourselves, to calm ourselves, to take time for rest, and to work toward healing ourselves. In Western thinking if we are in pain, we run to the doctor or the drug store to stop the pain. Once the pain is gone, we are glad, but rarely are we willing to think about the joy of being pain free. To be aware that we are pain free is to be mindful of what we have at the moment. To accept being free of pain is something we should honor. I will relate a personal story relevant to this example. For several years I have had severe pain in my right knee when I was driving my car. On one trip I would stop about every 50 miles to get out of the car and walk around it. That seemed to reduce the pain although it returned. On a recent trip to California I picked up a rental car at the San Francisco airport to drive north to Sonoma County although I did have to stop in downtown San Francisco to pick up the ashes of my sister which I was taking to our city of origin for internment. The pain became excruciating and I was hardly able to move around the next day. When I returned home, I finally reached a point of decision. I went to my physician asking if I should have a knee reconstruction. He assured me I did not need that and had me visit an Orthopedic Surgeon who took X-rays and showed me that I had plenty of ligament left and I did not need any surgery. Yet the pain persisted until one day I realized I had to do something. I have long legs and have always driven with my right leg canted to the right to avoid the steering wheel while I drove. I tried keeping my right leg straight up and down. I even added a cushion to raise my butt to ease my leg under the steering wheel. Within two months the pain was totally gone. I had believed that I would be doomed for life to live with that awful pain in my right knee. Now I thank the Holy Spirit for my recovery. But this experience taught me something even at this late date in my life: I can do things to change my life if I only look deeply and try to alter my actions.

As an end to this discussion of Buddhism, most of the teachings of the Buddha are to aid us to reach a state of peace, or in the final stages, what is called Nirvana. For those of you aware of the work of Maslow and his hierarchy of needs, his most advanced stage of goal seeking is described as reaching Self-actualization. Here again we can see that commonality of the Eastern notion of Nirvana, the ultimate state of peace for which we strive but few will ever reach, and the notion of Self-actualization which in Maslow's scheme is an ideal state toward which we strive but few will ever reach. Let us be reminded of the teachings of Jesus who stressed living free of the wants and needs of many people and even to relinquish the desire for material goods. Just as Jesus taught, the Buddhist monks travel around teaching their enlightenment but taking along their begging bowl with which to attain their daily bread.

# CHAPTER TEN

# TO GIVE IS TO RECEIVE

## THE THIRD PRINCIPLE OF ATTITUDINAL HEALING:

The principle is:

*"Giving and receiving are the same.* When our attention is on giving and joining with others, fear is removed and we accept healing for ourselves."

This principle can be interpreted in several ways. When I first encountered this principle I thought immediately of family members who were quick to give to others but were reluctant to accept from others. A similar idea stems from the practice of record keeping such that when someone invites you to a dinner, you make a note that you owe them a dinner. A similar example is when you are eating out with friends or family members, your spouse expects you to pay the bill almost every time. I believe that to accept a gift from someone is to honor them and all you need is to say thank you. Just as when you offer a gift to someone, you can ask that they accept it without any sense of owing you something in return.

Jampolsky offers a different slant on this principle. He wrote that your giving love to someone else does not take anything from you. In fact, sharing love will often result in others sharing love with you. As with accepting material gifts we could accept love unconditionally and expect to return that love unconditionally. In his words, Jampolsky wrote: "By being open to love we make ourselves open to giving love to others." Susan Trout in her book *To See Differently* (1990) wrote about two sorts of people whom she described as givers and takers.

- Givers are those who are martyrs and are always there to lend a helping hand.
- Takers are those who are always on the lookout for a gift from others.

She takes this principle to mean that we should avoid being either givers or takers, but be sharers, those who are comfortable giving and receiving. She pointed out that people who are the givers set themselves up as being strong while the other person is weak. It also means that when the giver does in fact need help, there is no one ready to offer it. Takers, in contrast to givers, present themselves as needy and lacking. When we can balance giving and receiving we work toward healing.

In couples therapy the term over-functioning is used to describe a spouse who takes the major responsibility for one or more aspects of a marriage relationship. The one who does it all takes over the tasks involved thereby ensuring they are completed but not allowing for a balance of responsibilities in the marriage. The one that over functions does not balance giving and receiving in daily practice.

# THE BUDDHA'S TEACHING ABOUT EQUALITY IN RELATIONSHIPS.

From the Buddhist perspective, this principle is most closely related to the Buddhist teaching of Right Action. From *The Heart of the Buddha's Teaching* Thich Nhat Hanh wrote that:

> "The Second Mindfulness Training is about generosity: Aware of the suffering caused by exploitation, social injustice, stealing and oppression, I am committed to cultivating loving kindness and learning ways to work for the well-being of people, animals, plants, and minerals.
>
> I will practice generosity by sharing my time, energy, and material resources with those who are in real need."
> (Page 94)

Teaching to be generous, he continued, is more than not taking what are others or exploiting others, but to live in a manner that can bring about social justice and well-being of your society. When we learn to live knowing that we have enough to meet our daily needs, we will have material to share with others.

A comprehensive discussion of generosity is in the Lama Surya Das' *Buddha Is As Buddha Does.* Chapter One is The Transcendental Gift of Generosity which is an extensive review of the teachings of Eastern religion about giving and receiving. The chapter contains a series of short verses which are a resource worth repeating.

> "May I perfect the sublime virtue of generosity, which
> liberates and releases craving, grasping, and attachment,
> and brings joyous contentment?

A major teaching of Buddhism is to forgo longing and coveting things for themselves. This teaching is similar to that of Jesus who taught that one should not amass wealth. *Dana* is the Sanskrit word for what in English we would call generosity although it can mean much more. Dana ". . . is similar to the Christian concept of *caritas* (Latin for 'charity')." This practice means selflessly bestowing compassion and benefits to others without expecting any return.

From Lao Tzu we find KNOWING HOW TO BE GENEROUS.

> The sage accumulates nothing,
> but the more he does for others
> the greater his existence;
> the more he gives to others,
> the greater his abundance.

Near the end to Das' chapter on generosity, he brought into play the concept of Tonglen which is a meditation for becoming more generous. Commenting on Tonglen, Mother Teresa spoke of us as follows:

"The problem with this world is that we draw our family circle too small."

Let's apply this notion to modern countries that are unwilling to accept that their country is now multicultural and that all people of their country are equal to all others and should be treated as such. If we apply giving and receiving to all others, we will make no distinctions among people as they are all the same in the eyes of the Holy Spirit.

About Tonglen, Das wrote the following:

> "The practice of *Tonglen* (literally, 'giving-receiving'),
> brought to Tibet by Master Atisha in the eleventh century,
> is an ideal one for opening up, facing fear and difficulty,
> recognizing the dreamlike nature of things, and expanding
> our capacity to be generous. It helps us let go of our isolated
> self-clinging and transforms our egocentric perspective,
> step-by-step, into a universal one, filled with unconditional
> love and oneness."

Perhaps this book should be about oneness rather than fusion, although I do not believe these are truly separate concepts as they are one.

# CHAPTER ELEVEN

# RELEASING THE PAST AND THE FUTURE

## THE FOURTH PRINCIPLE OF ATTITUDINAL HEALING:

*"We can let go of the past and the future.* We experience inner peace when we let go of our attachments to the painful past and the fearful future and learn to live in the present."

Many of us are dedicated to attachments to our past and use the past to justify our current situation. A common statement is something like this. "I was born into a dysfunctional family." "My father always criticized what I did." "I could never meet my mother's standards." All of these statements are actually false. Once I was listening to PBS and heard a woman say that a dysfunctional family was not a diagnostic category. I was certain she was Anne Schaef, as I knew her work. She said "All families are in some extent dysfunctional." You should not try to put blame on your family for where you are today. Rather than taking responsibility for our present actions, we blame a distant parent, ex-lover, the government, etc.

This is not an easy principle because it contains several distinct elements. First is the notion that our past was painful. We have to understand before we move further that the past is a fiction which we create through our memories. We do not actually have a past, but our present memories of the past. Related to this point is that not all past was painful, but we tend to hang on to those parts that were painful. When we do so, we use those memories as an excuse for our actions and reactions today. For example, a person in a group once said she wanted her father to love her. When queried we found that her father had passed away many years ago but she still was struggling with her feelings that her father did not truly love her. There was nothing she could do now that would make her father love her that she had not done earlier. She should let go of the past and move on. When we are willing to accept that the past is our creation and that it cannot be the cause of things now, we can readily let it go.

The next element of this principle is that the future is fearful. The only reason we fear the future is that we expect it to recapitulate the past. The woman who sought her father's love cannot continue to do so in the future as her father is dead. Imagine you were to find a diary written by your mother upon her death that had negative things to say about you. My recommendation is to burn it! Later we will discuss the role for forgiveness in our lives and we will find that by forgiving we will no longer allow a hurtful event in the past to control and influence our present situation.

The most important element of the fifth principle is the one in the middle, that the only time there is, is between the past and the future or the present moment. When we realize all we have is that present moment, we will stop looking to our memory of the past and not look ahead to an unknown future, but focus on now.

Jampolsky wrote about this in paragraph one of page 107 in *Teach Only Love.*

> "The present is the only time we can choose between love and fear. When we fret about the past, or worry about what to do in the future, we accomplish nothing. And yet, our mental habit of reliving the past and rehearsing what is to come generates various forms of pain. A mental shift into the present helps remove the source of misery."

At the end of his book *Illusions* Richard Bach wrote that "Everything in this book may be wrong." Bach very clearly allowed us to decide whether to believe what he wrote. Jampolsky did the same with the following three statements near the end of Chapter Eleven about the Fourth Principle:

- If we fear the world, we will hesitate to do anything without considering all the consequences.
- As a baby struggles to learn to walk, she never pauses to analyze why she just fell down.
- Learning to respond to now is all there is to learn . . . .

## THE TEACHING OF THE BUDDHA
## ABOUT OUR PAST AND FUTURE

An aspect of the enlightened master is that he or she never gives a direct set of rules by which to live. In western culture we find many examples of written instructions on how to do things. I often ask a class if they can learn how to swim by reading a book and taking a multiple-choice test on the book? The answer should be obvious, yet western education is based on the principle of reading, memorizing, and testing on the readings. The Tao or way is not taught from a book but can only be learned by practice and experience. The master sets the example for the novice to note and practice. In short, in the Eastern way one demonstrates by example and offers aid through the practice of meditation and being mindful. There is no set of statements about letting go of the past and future, but through the practice of meditation and being present in the moment, one will be able to let go of the past and to ignore the future. The Buddha also taught his students to avoid attachments by not clinging to the past. When clinging to the past ceases, much pain of the past and fear of the future ceases.

For example, a teaching on the *End of Clinging*. (*The Teachings of the Buddha*, Jack Kornfield):

The person "who dwells contemplating the sorrow of all things that make for clinging, craving ceases, when craving ceases, clinging ceases; when clinging ceases, the process of becoming ceases . . . Thus the entire mass of suffering ceases."

One other teaching is about abandoning sorrow. When the enlightened one spoke of how sorrows could be avoided by not paying attention to them, one of his students asked:

"What causes of sorrow should be abandoned by not paying attention to them?" The answer was that: "They are those things which, when dwelt upon, give rise to sorrow and which increase existing sorrow."

Thus the Buddhist seeks to lose any attachments to things in the past that cause sorrow, in the same way that a teacher of *Attitudinal Healing* encourages his students to let go of the past.

From The Noble Eightfold Path we find Right Mindfulness. As presented by Thich Nhat Hanh in *The Heart of the Buddha's Teaching* (Page 65), "Right Mindfulness is the energy that brings us back to the present moment." We often allow ourselves to drift away to the past or the future; when we practice right mindfulness we are in the present moment, and when we are in the present moment we have to let go of the past and of the future. No matter how long one studies and practices the Eightfold Path, he or she will often lose the way and drift afar from right mindfulness. Then we must redirect ourselves to the way.

This is not wrong but is only a reminder that we have to refresh ourselves from time to time. Hanh wrote further that "Mindfulness is remembering to come back to the present moment . . . . The First Miracles of Mindfulness is to be present and able to touch deeply the blue sky, the flower, and the smile of our child."

I am saddened when I walk along a pathway and see individuals either talking on their cell phone or listening to their IPOD. These persons are not using their time wisely as when one walks a pathway, he or she needs to see the birds, the flowers, and the trees to be mindful. Western culture seems to work so hard at keeping us from the Eightfold Path and from Mindfulness. There is nothing in our culture that prevents us from being mindful. When one begins to practice being mindful, that person will gain great rewards for the spirit.

Love, Thick Nhat Hanh wrote (*The Heart of Buddha's Teaching*), is maitri in Sanskrit which also can be translated as loving kindness.

He commented that some Buddhist teachers avoid the word love as being dangerous and instead use loving kindness. Hanh prefers the term love although he wrote "Words sometimes get sick and we have to heal them. We have been using the word "love" to mean appetite or desire, as in "I love hamburgers." We have to use language more carefully. "Love" is a beautiful word; we have to restore its meaning." He wrote further that in Buddhism the primary translation of the term love is friendship. As in a marriage that lasts many years, we find that friendship is the factor that keeps the marriage intact. Too often one goes off searching for the lost love that never was.

# CHAPTER TWELVE

# WHY NOT NOW?

## THE FIFTH PRINCIPLE OF ATTITUDINAL HEALING:

As Jampolsky wrote: "The present is the only time we can choose between love and fear." We might amplify this statement as the only time we have is now—this instant. But, we confuse ourselves with memories of the past that may be fearful and by recalling the past we tend to project it onto our future. If we want to seek love rather than fear, we must do so in the present moment. The Principle is:

> "*Now is the only time there is*. Pain, grief, depression, guilt, and other forms of fear disappear when the mind is focused on loving peace on this instant."

Since the past is our creation, we can change the recollection of the past or simply let it go away. The easiest way to let the past go is to focus on the present. When we do so, we will not be able to think about the past. By letting the past go, we will avoid being fearful of the future, as we only fear the future because our memories of the past will predict that the future will be like the past.

Caroline Myss in *Why People Don't Heal* (1997) tells a story about a friend Mary who was not able to heal from her wound due incest in her family. Caroline was visiting a center in Scotland to conduct a workshop and was expecting important persons to be arriving at the airport who would need transportation. At lunch with some friends Mary walked by and Caroline asked her if she was free the next day to help bring visitors to the center. Mary got very upset and said she could not be free as that was the day her incest group would be meeting. Later, when alone with Mary, Caroline asked her why she thought it necessary to tell the luncheon group about her support group. Mary had so strongly identified herself as an incest victim that she would not let go of that part of her past. In Caroline's work with victims of incest she found that letting go of the hurt was the best way to heal, and she thought that Mary was not working to heal her wounds.

Caroline also wrote about the seductive power of wounds. When she formed a new group, during the first few sessions participants seemed to try to outdo each other in recalling their wounds. Caroline saw that clinging to wounds was not helping people heal. In terms of *The Course* it was the ego of these participants that was making them dwell on their past wounds. In terms of the energy people expend in speaking about their wounds, all that energy could go to working in the present moment rather than holding onto the past. This section will end with a quote from Caroline Myss: "One of the main beliefs that I want you to adopt in order to heal your life or illness is a belief in the importance of forgiveness. Forgiveness frees up the energy necessary for healing. I will present suggestions on how to go about forgiving—or letting go of—the past, and will give you new rituals and invocations for helping you see your present life Symbolically, bolster your personal energy, connect you with Divine energy, and help you heal."

*William H. Calhoun, Ph. D.*

# THE TEACHINGS OF THE BUDDHA ABOUT BEING IN THE MOMENT.

Caroline Myss spans the east and west in her work and writings. Much of what she will teach can be phrased as a merger of east and west. Caroline Myss is a medical intuitive who can diagnose disorders by evaluating a person's aura. She explained what she did:

> "As a medical intuitive, I describe for people the nature of their physical diseases as well as the energetic dysfunctions that are present within their bodies. I read the energy field that permeates and surrounds the body, picking up information . . ."

She refers to her field as energy medicine in which she offers to treat the body as well as the spirit. Energy medicine is actually quite an old field of knowledge as the principles and techniques were known to the ancient Hindu, Chinese, and shamanic healers. Caroline added: "What I believe is new is my correlation of Eastern spiritual ideas of the chakras with Western spiritual truths and ethics to create a new language of energy." Caroline Myss uses energy medicine to help a person realign the mind and body into a unified whole. When the mind and body are unified, you are living in the moment.

Thich Nhat Hanh in *The Heart of the Buddha's Teaching* wrote about Right Thinking as it relates to the issue of living in the now.

> "Right Thinking reflects the way things are. Wrong thinking causes us to see in an 'upside-down way'. But to practice Right Thinking is not easy. Our mind is often

thinking about one thing while our body is doing another. Mind and body are not unified."

In Caroline's work she uses energy medicine adopted from eastern teachings to realign the mind and body.

Jon Kabat-Zinn offered his advice for Capturing Your Moments in his book *Wherever You Go There You Are.* "The best way to capture moments is to pay attention. This is how we cultivate mindfulness." He offered the following for out use:

> "You can easily observe the mind's habit of escaping from the present moment for yourself.
> Just try to keep your attention focused on any object for even a short period of time. You will find that to cultivate mindfulness, you may have to remember over and over again to be awake and aware. We do this by reminding ourselves to look, to feel, to be. It's that simple . . . checking in from moment to moment, sustaining awareness across a stretch of timeless moments, being here now."

Jack Kornfield quoted from the Dhammapada this bit of advice:

> *Look within.*
> *Be still.*
> *Free from fear and attachment, Know the*
> *sweet joy of living in the way.*

One final reminder that is true for all the sections of this chapter:

> "The Buddha gave a wide variety of instructions, and if some of them help us to live better, to solve our problems, and become kinder, then we are free to practice them. There is no need to call ourselves Buddhists. The purpose of the Buddha's teachings is to benefit us, and if putting some of them into practice helps us live more peacefully with ourselves and others, that is what's important."

# CHAPTER THIRTEEN

# FORGIVE RATHER THAN JUDGE

## THE SIXTH PRINCIPLE OF
## ATTITUDINAL HEALING:

The Sixth Principle of Attitudinal Healing is about letting go of past hurts and to withhold judgment to seek peace. The full principle is:

> *"We can learn to love ourselves and others by forgiving rather than judging.* Forgiveness is the way to true health and happiness. When we choose to see everyone as a teacher of forgiveness, each moment gives us an opportunity for happiness, peace, and love."

The act of forgiving is to let go of the past and to move onward. It must be emphasized that the process of forgiving is about yourself, not that you are telling the one who hurt you that what he did was alright. A classic example of forgiving was written by Debbie Morris in her book *Forgiving the Dead Man Walking* (2010). Debbie was one of two girls held hostage for two days and repeatedly raped by a group of three men who had escaped for a prison in Mississippi. The other girl was killed and the person featured in the film *Dead*

*Man Walking* was Willie who was sentenced to die for his part in the murder of the girl. Debbie was willing to share a very intimate part of her life with the reader through her book. Her point was that she did not seek revenge against Willie, and was not interested in his execution. She was working to put her life back together. She was a high school student at the time of her kidnapping and rape. She was offered counseling and did not take up on the offer. Because she might be needed to testify, the authorities limited her school hours. After the trial was over she tried to resume her life, but had two bouts with alcoholism, a marriage and divorce and alienation from her mother. She later entered AA and in the final session her mother attended. At this session Debbie was able to state that she wanted to forgive her mother for being out the night she was kidnapped. The point of this story is that forgiveness is about you, not about someone else. If you choose to remain a victim and use that as an excuse for your issues today, you are not letting go of the past and you are not forgiving yourself to allow for healing.

Jampolsky noted that the root meaning of the verb to forgive means to let go. We often make the error of thinking that by forgiving we are letting the person who harmed us think that what she did was okay. By forgiving we let go of the past, and can begin a new life as Debbie did with her mother. At the end of her book she is married, has earned a master's degree in education, has a rewarding career, has a daughter, and has re-established a relationship with her mother. This outcome was not easy to obtain as it took her nineteen years from the time of the rape to the time of forgiveness with a divorce, job loss, alcoholism, and a lot of personal judgment along the way. I would think of Debbie as enlightened through her experience and her willingness to tell her story akin to the way used by the Buddha.

She did not lecture or tell her reader what to do, but she shared her personal experience for others to learn about and profit from her experience.

> From *The Course* (Page 354) "To forgive is merely to remember only the loving thoughts you gave in the past, and those that we've given you. All the rest must be forgotten. Forgiveness is a selective remembering, based not on your selection."

Continuing:

"The real world is attained simply by the complete forgiveness of the old, the world you see without forgiveness.

"All this beauty will rise to bless your sight as you look upon the world with forgiving eyes. For forgiveness literally transforms vision, and lets you see the real world reaching quietly and gently across chaos, removing all illusions that had twisted your perception and fixed it on the past."

It may seem on first blush that to hold a grudge against someone who harmed you in the past is normal. Many persons hold grudges which they offer as reasons for their current actions, feelings, and thoughts. Recall that Caroline Myss wrote about a friend she spoke with while attending a workshop. When her friend approached her Caroline asked if she could be free next week to escort a friend to the workshop. Mary, her friend, reacted emotionally mentioning that she had an incest support group on that day and she could not possibly miss that meeting. Later Caroline asked Mary why she felt she needed to tell about her incest to those at the table and why was she holding on to this situation after all this time. This example is only one of many where a person holds onto a history of distress. In the Buddhists' language, she is clinging to the past and she needs to let it go.

## PRINCIPLE SIX FROM THE BUDDHIST PERSPECTIVE

The Buddhist way seems to be proactive rather than reactive as the teachings of the Buddha are intended to enter into your life at an early age and to be practiced repeatedly as one works along the way and toward enlightenment. The act of forgiveness is mostly based on some event that occurred early in one's life before the individual had begun to study the Buddhist way. In Western practice interventions such as psychotherapy are brought to bear on the past and hurtful events which occurred in the past. There is an intermediate phase in this process which involves letting go which is a theme in both Western and Eastern teachings. Jon Kabat-Zinn wrote in his book *Wherever You Go There You Are* about letting go:

> "Letting go means just what it says. It's an invitation to cease clinging to anything—whether it is an idea, a thing, an event, a particular time, or view, or desire. It is a conscious decision to release with full acceptance into stream of present moments as they are unfolding. To let go means to give up coercing, resisting, or struggling, in exchange for something more powerful and wholesome which comes out of allowing things to be

as they are without getting caught in your attraction to or rejection of them, in the intrinsic stickiness of wanting, of liking and disliking. It's akin to letting your palm open to unhand something you have been holding on to."

Kabat-Jon continued by reminding us that not only do we hold things tightly in our hands, we also hold things tightly in our minds.

Jack Kornfield quoted from the *Dhammapada* about hate and joy.

> In this world
> Hate never yet dispelled hate. Only love dispels hate.
> This is the law,

> Live in joy, In love,
> Even among those who hate.

Additional wisdom from the *Dhammapada* as mentioned in Wikidepia include the following:

> All that we are is the result of what we have thought . . .
> Do not speak harshly to anybody . . .
> One is one's own refuge, what other refuge can there be??
> Rouse yourself, be diligent, in Dhamma faring well.
> Who dwells in Dhamma's happy in this birth and the next.

This is a very old document written in Sanskrit and later in Pali. These verses were attributed to the Buddha some years before the birth of Jesus. To quote from Wikipedia ". . . the Dhammapada makes the Buddhist way of life available to anyone . . ."

What we find in these passages are the instructions for practice. It is not that you need to know the words, but that you know that the practice of these suggestions will lead you to the way. One of the greatest things about the Eastern philosophies and religions is that they are about how to conduct your life in order to be at peace. As the last two lines say, "Subdue yourself, and discover your master."

Notice how often the term love comes into these verses. While *Attitudinal Healing* begins with the concept of love as being what one should teach; in Eastern thinking, love is everywhere. By giving up hatred you will find love. When you have learned to follow these teachings, then you are ready to teach others. You can help them find the way and thereby find peace and love.

# CHAPTER FOURTEEN

# FIND LOVE, NOT FAULT

## THE SEVENTH PRINCIPLE OF ATTITUDINAL HEALING:

B ecoming a love finder is very important for persons living in Western culture as we apply the notions that come from the capitalist economic system where people seek power over others in order to advance their own position. When we stress competition over cooperation, we all lose. Therefore, Jampolsky adopted his Seventh principle.

> *"We can become love-finders rather than faultfinders.*
> Regardless of what another person's behavior may be, we can always choose to see only the light of love in that person."

By way of introduction to this statement Jampolsky stated that this principle ". . . presents a clear choice we must all eventually make if we wish to know lasting peace and love."

There are two different ideas in this principle:

- We can become love finders.
- We try not to find fault with others.

*The Course* has as a central theme that we are to be love and our role in life is to find love in ourselves and others. It is assumed that when we focus on finding love we will automatically not find fault. Let's see if that will hold true as we examine this principle.

Jampolsky wrote "All egos are alike." That is a very strong statement, and before we can examine it, we must understand what we mean by Ego. The term ego in Latin means the I, or the self.

When Freud first wrote about what has become the ego he used the German term for I which is Ich. At this point the I was neutral as it referred to our sense of self which seems self-evident. Yet, when the Americans began to adopt Freud's ideas, the word Ich was altered to the word Ego. This may appear to be a minor point, although you will find that persons consider the word Ego to mean much more that the simple concept of I or self.

In *A Course in Miracles* the term ego takes on a specific meaning that we must understand before we tackle this principle. From *The Course* we find:

"Consciousness is correctly identified as the domain of the ego." "The ego is a wrong-minded attempt to perceive yourself as you wish to be, rather than as you are."

*The Course* presents the ego in a very negative manner, which needs to be recognized but not simply accepted. In modern thinking the ego, or the sense of self, is a necessary first step in the development of the personality. Hence, it not inherently bad, although if one does not move beyond the ego and remains in that stage of development, the consequences will be poor (Calhoun, 2006). It is desirable to move beyond the ego stage of development, but one must move through that stage to achieve the higher state.

*The Course* defines the ego as attacking others and judging others as a way to defend itself from attack. This statement gets us to the point of Principle Seven, which is to set aside or move beyond the ego in order to eliminate judging as a common practice and thereby move on to finding love. In Western religion the God of the Hebrews tended to be a God of judgment rather than a God of love. It was only when we encountered Jesus do we see the emphasis shift to giving and seeking love as a major goal of religious practice in the west.

## THE BUDDHA'S TEACHING ABOUT FINDING LOVE

As mentioned Eastern religious practice is proactive. In Buddhism you are taught from an early age about suffering and how to follow steps to deal with suffering. You are also taught the Eight Noble Truths. The fact that you are taught these practices before you have lived very long suggests that the practices of the one seeking enlightenment will ward off or prevent many ills from confounding the person. This is an ideal situation and in many cases people have come to a Monk with questions about eliminating a problem or counteracting something which has befallen the seeker. But, if you begin to practice the teachings you will be prepared to deal with issues as they arise. In Western religions people often come to the teacher with questions about getting something from God or having God intervene in some situation.

As we begin with this perspective, we will find that many of the teachings of the Buddha are to set aside the self or the ego. One of the many teachings offers the idea of No Self, or the absence of an Ego. I do believe that Western and Eastern people are very much alike and a sense of self is necessary in the early years of one's development. But I also believe that Easterners are correct in seeking to move beyond the self into a state of No Self. From Kornfield's *Teachings of the Buddha* we find:

> "The instructed disciple of the Noble Ones does not regard material shape as self, or self as having material shape, or material shape as being in the self, or the self as being in material shape."

The enlightened Buddhist will not have the experience of Ego as we see in Western thinking, and the entire role of the teachings are about love rather than enhancing the goals of the Ego. Standard teachings of child development assume that all persons will reach an ego stage and most will move through that stage to a new level of development. In the competitive world of modern business a strong Ego is valuable. The emergence of the sense of self or the ego tends to occur during the teenage years and in some cases the individual will remain locked in the ego stage. There are two points about this observation. First, we have noted that many persons in the west experience what is termed a midlife crisis as they reach the mid-years. This is the time when the Ego is no longer dominant and the person is trying to adjust to the new situation. Therapists who work with these clients help the person learn to set aside the ego and move on to a more enlightened state. It is worthy of note that Buddhist monks normally do not start training until the age of sixteen. The classic example is that of the Dalai Lama who begins training at that age by which time the young man has reached the ego stage and the next step is moving beyond the ego. In American culture today young men tend to continue in the ego stage for many years as we have extended the adolescent span well into the twenties with continued education expected.

My point is that in the Eastern teachings it is assumed the individual has developed an adequate ego that will allow him or her to enter into serious education into the Eastern Philosophy which goes beyond the ego stage of life.

One final quote from the Buddha:

> The Buddha said: "If outsiders speak against me, the Teaching, or the Order, you should not be angry for that would prevent your own self-conquest. Similarly if they praise us. But you should find out what is false or true, and acknowledge the fact. And even in praise it is only of trifling matters that an unconverted man might speak of me."

# CHAPTER FIFTEEN

# CHOOSING PEACE

## THE EIGHTH PRINCIPLE OF ATTITUDINAL HEALING

This principle is about bringing peace to our mind without regard to what is happening elsewhere. The Principle is:

> *"We can be peaceful inside regardless of what is happening outside.* Despite the chaos in our lives, we can choose to be peaceful, knowing that we are connected and sustained by our loving, peaceful source."

Jampolsky wrote that according to *The Course* the ego teaches that the past will determine the future, and the ego does this in order to sustain fear of the future. By recognizing that love will counter fear when we think in terms of how we can love ourselves and others, we will circumvent fear. One axiom in this process is that as we conduct our lives we must keep reminding ourselves to think and teach only love.

The ego teaches that we can blame our problems on external events such as our childhood, a failed marriage, or our inability to get and keep a good job. *The Course* teaches us that we can counter the ego by letting go of the past and realizing that we can be peaceful if we work to be peaceful. There are numerous events in our everyday life that we can use to verify this principle. There is a scale of life events that mentions serious issues such as graduation, marriage, going to jail, losing a parent, suffering divorce—major life events. But for us it is the small, daily events that happen to us which matter. We are not considering major life events which occur rarely in one's life. For example, you ran out of tooth paste this morning, your morning paper was late, you could not find any sweetener for you tea, and your car was hard to start. More serious, there was a traffic jam on the highway making you late to work. Let's start with a traffic jam. As you slow your car and come to a stop, focus on your music on the radio. If you are listening to a talk show, turn it off! You do not need to hear anything bad. Look at the person next to you and wave and smile. She will probably wave back, and both of you will feel better. Think how many times you are frustrated in any given day, and ask yourself why you notice these things. Let the other person get ahead of you in line at the bank. When you cannot find a close parking place, think of how nice a brief walk would be. Do not carry your cell phone into a store or restaurant. Be mindful. One of the many stories in *Chicken Soup for the Soul* is about a man who arrives home from work, parks his car, gets out, and walks out to a tree in his front yard; he places his hand on the tree for a moment. When asked why he did this, he said: "I hang up my troubles from today on the tree so I can ignore them when I am with my family. In the morning I will come and pick them up again. But tonight I am free." This man has learned how to be peaceful inside regardless of what happened to him during the day.

Western courts of law are based on the notion of intent. Our courts make two serious errors. First, they rely on what they call eyewitness testimony, even recognizing that research shows that such testimony is often faulty. Second, they look for a motive for the action or crime. No one, not even the perpetrator, will ever know the motive. Or, there may not be one. Psychologists have major theories about motivation and have done numerous studies of motives. Yet, when it comes down to it, all we will ever know is what the person did. In a chapter on motivation the author spent many pages writing about research on the theories only to end the chapter with the following statement: "If an operant occurs, it was motivated." An operant is a technical term but literally means any voluntary action emitted by an organism. Therefore, the statement above means that if an action or sequence of actions occurs, they were motivated. The crucial word here is when. We only can know that the action was motivated when we know it happened. Suggesting that the action was motivated adds nothing to the observation that the action occurred.

To make this point clearer I will relate a common experience in my life. I have a friend who often asks me to take him to the airport where he is to catch a plane. There are at least three ways to get to the airport from his home, and I pick one of those with little thought. As we are traveling along, he will ask me why I took this route. I do not know, but I did. That is all I know, and that is all he can know. For fun, I might say I did it to tease him, I like to vary my routes, I mentally tossed a coin, or some other idle thought. But the fact remains that I took the route and it will get us to the airport. His attempt to ascertain my motivation for taking the route will not succeed. The point of this example is to demonstrate that all we ever can know is that I took a specific route to the airport. Why does not matter. In one Attitudinal Healing group we tried to adopt the notion we would not ever say "I should have . . . ." The fact is that one cannot go back and change things. What is done is done.

This principle tells us that we can influence how we experience our life, only if we believe we have, and therefore, we can change how we feel. We can work to be peaceful inside, regardless of what is happening outside. But, we have to practice and practice to ensure this will happen.

## THE BUDDHA'S TEACHING ABOUT INNER PEACE

This principle underlies the teaching of all Eastern religions. Recall the Buddhist prayer at the beginning of this part of the book. The prayer asks that all of us may come to be at peace in the world. Recognizing that there are many bad things in the world, we still are in need of inner peace and harmony. If one were to take the first seven principles and seek a common core, it would be that by accepting that we can offer love to everyone, and by so doing we will find peace, this principle is redundant. Being redundant is fine as in any teachings it is usual to repeat the lessons over and over as we often will forget them in our day-to-day lives. When the Christian God told us to rest on the seventh day, he did not mean for us to forget the lessons, but to stop and think about the teachings. Of the Eastern traditions, meditation is the method whereby we come to remind ourselves of the teachings and refresh our commitment to practice those teachings.

Das in *Buddha Is As Buddha Does* offered this thought. "What's involved in creating an inner state of equanimity and inclusiveness?

The more important element is getting beyond the notion of a separate egoistic self and instead becoming one in our hearts and minds with the world around us, with all its myriad forms and dreamlike manifestations."

Many of us living today believe they are the first people to experience a world of frenzy, anger, and hate. If one were to study history deeply, it would be evident that such events have been a part of life from the very beginning. We will find that most Eastern religions grew out of a period of war and chaos from which enlightened ones tried to end this era with a semblance of peace. These teachings anticipated Jampolsky's development of principle eight. In no way does that mean that *Attitudinal Healing* cannot offer a lesson to today's people.

Thick Nhat Hanh has been cited many times in this book and his experience is relevant to the issue of inner peace amid chaos. He was a Buddhist monk in Vietnam during the period of the war and saw many acts of violence as a part of that war. He was true to his calling and was able to set aside the chaos of the war to try and teach his message to those who would listen. In a sense he practiced the Eighth Principle as he was living in a time a great chaos but he sought to find inner peace.

Following his teachings, we can find peace inside in spite of what is going on outside.

# CHAPTER SIXTEEN

# ALL RELATIONSHIPS ARE EQUAL

## THE NINTH PRINCIPLE OF
## ATTITUDINAL HEALING:

T his principle is easily stated as *"We are students and teachers to each other."*

As a college professor I can relate to this principle in a unique manner. Jampolsky emphasized how the people at his Center are treated equally. The full principle is:

> *"We are students and teachers to each other.* Peace
> comes to us when we recognize and demonstrate that all
> our relationships are equal."

I find the first sentence of this principle to be the most profound. I do believe that treating everyone as equal will foster the inter-action among various individuals regardless of credentials or ages. But, I first have a story to tell.

I have been teaching for about twenty-five years when our college adopted a new type of course called the capstone. This course was envisioned as bringing together the material in the major field for students in the latter semesters of their college career. I began with the naïve idea that I would use a high level, introductory textbook of psychology. I quickly realized that the students did not want that. Thus I began to listen to the students' comments and started using books such as Richard Bach's *Illusions,* Oliver Sachs *The Man Who Mistook his Wife for a Hat,* Kathleen Norris' *The Cloister Walk,* M Scott Peck's *The Road Less Traveled,* etc. These books were highly readable and contained significant messages for the students. The response was very positive. In addition I made a point of sitting at the side of the large table, rather than the head or foot and at the same level as the students to abide by the notion of equality. I started doing this work long before I came upon Attitudinal Healing and this principle only verified what I had found was that I could learn from my students when I am open and willing. In fact, where there are thirty students and one teacher, the students will have greater knowledge to offer me that I will have to offer them.

When we approach a person with the openness and willingness to listen to what they have to offer, before offering our view, we are being mindful. While in a small group one member offers an example of a problem, do not try to offer one of your own. Listen to what they have to say and acknowledge that. When you pause and truly listen, you will gain empathy for that person. Being a good listener is being mindful. Experienced physicians and psychotherapists soon learn to listen to their patients or clients and glean from them bits and pieces of knowledge which they may not even realize they know. You want to summarize what you believe you have learned for your patient or client to confirm the information. Do not offer to solve a problem, but lead them to find a solution on their own. You teach best by example rather than through direct instruction.

Richard Bach has written many books but his most mystical one was titled *Illusions*. Bach subtitled his book as The Adventures of a Reluctant Messiah who was Don Shimoda in the book. Shimoda taught Richard from the *Messiah's Handbook* which contained many interesting sayings from which the following comes:

> *Learning is finding out*
> *what you already know.*
> *Doing is demonstrating that*
> *you know it.*
> *Teaching is reminding others*
> *that they know just as well as you.*
> *You are all learners, doers, teachers.*

## THE TEACHINGS OF THE BUDDHA ABOUT TEACHING AND LEARNING

Most Eastern thinking alludes to teaching and learning but they do not specifically address this issue. They write about meditation as a means of gaining inner wisdom and they stress how the novice can learn by observing the master and later practicing what the master does. Most teaching done by the Lamas is through example and practice. If you are to learn how to breathe, you do not read a book and practice one, two, and three. You watch the master and hear him speak as:

> "I breathe in, and I feel peace.
> As I breathe out I feel love, etc."

Jampolsky wrote about how we are teachers and learners to each other. The Buddhists would agree that no single master knows everything, and the seeker who is on the path will accept whatever wisdom and knowledge he or she can obtain along the way. Jon Kabat-Zinn wrote *Wherever You Go There You Are* in which he described the Buddhists teachings. In one section he wrote about having a child.

> "Becoming a parent clearly was going to be the biggest transformation of my adult life so far.
> To do it well would demand the greatest clarity of view and the greatest letting go and letting be
> I had ever been challenged with." (Pages 248-249.)

For him, this would be a great learning experience, and he would learn from the child and the child would learn from him. Later he added: "I felt that parenting was nothing short of a perfect opportunity to deepen mindfulness, if I could let the children and the family become my teachers, and remember to recognize and listen carefully to the lessons in living which would be coming fast and furiously."

My experience of becoming a grandparent was a great opportunity for me to watch the child grow. When I was a parent I was often too busy or distracted to watch my sons as they learned, but with grandchildren, I had the opportunity to observe their learning. I will share a story about my oldest granddaughter. She was born in China and was adopted by my son and daughter-in-law when she was about one year old. I watched her explore the world and saw how quickly she picked up on things. When she was about three years old we were seated on the patio of my son's home and he had a track with a child's car on rails. He would place his daughter in the car and send her rolling down the track. After several trips they stopped. I watched my granddaughter go into the house. I pictured her climbing the stairs to her bed room to get her baby, a doll about a foot tall. As I guessed, she re-appeared with the doll she called Baby in her arms and placed it in the car on the track and mimicking by son's actions eased the car down the track. For me this was a magnificent case of learning by example for a young child.

From a German philosopher comes one of the earliest examples where east and west meet. Eugen Herrigel spent the years of 1920 to 1924 teaching philosophy in Japan. He was interested in archery and asked a colleague to tutor him in archery. His friend at first declined as he had failed with an earlier western man. But with persistence by Herrigel his friend agreed. To start Herrigel was shown different bows and arrows and taught how to notch the bow and he was left on his own. After weeks of practice, Herrigel was ready to give up; he went to his friend to ask for help. The Master told him that "You cannot do it because you do not breathe right." He continued with instructions about breathing. "Press your breath down gently after breathing in, so that the abdominal wall is tightly stretched, and hold it therefore a while. Then breathe out as slowly and evenly as possible, and, after a short pause, draw a quick breath of air again— out and in continually, in a rhythm that will gradually settle itself. If it is done properly, you will feel the shooting becoming easier every day."

He added that ". . . through this breathing you will discover the source of all spiritual strength but will also cause this source to flow more abundantly, and to pour more easily through your limbs the more relaxed you are." With continued practice you will develop a rhythm that will become natural. At first it was difficult but eventually Herrigel become a proficient archer. His Master told him "A great

Master must also be a great teacher." These two things go hand in hand. Had he begun the lessons with breathing exercises, he would never have been able to convince his student to do the exercises. "You had to suffer shipwreck through your own efforts before you were ready to seize the lifebelt I threw you."

When Herrigel returned to Germany he wrote a long article about this experience and tried to foster the study of Zen Buddhism in Germany but we can see from our experience he did not make a significant impact. The typical westerner will hurry to shoot the first arrow and continue to do poorly only to blame the equipment and never learn the secret of the breathing exercises.

Kabat-Zinn commented further that this period in his life was like a retreat in which some periods were very difficult and some less so or even easy. He concluded by writing: "Through it all, the principle of looking at it as a meditation retreat and honoring the children and the family situation as my teachers has proven its primacy and value time and time again." Kabat-Zinn's writings which apply the lessons he learned in meditation retreats to parenting his child shows the general principles of teaching and learning that are inherent in Eastern teachings even though they are not explicitly mentioned. The master is never too old to learn something new, and the novice brings a fresh perspective to learning about the way and the middle path.

# CHAPTER SEVENTEEN

# BECOMING WHOLE

## THE TENTH PRINCIPLE OF ATTITUDINAL HEALING

This principle of attitudinal healing asks us to see the whole rather than the specific details of our lives. When we spend our time jumping from idea to idea, from item to item, or event to event, we are overlooking the big picture or the whole of our lives. This principle has several elements that may help us reach peace. The Principle is:

> *"We can focus on the whole of our lives rather than on the fragments.* It is an illusion to believe that our lives are separate from each other. Healing is focusing on our interconnectedness with each other and all living things."

The ego is constantly alert and watching for threats that it keeps us in a state of fear and confusion. When we stop letting our ego direct our attention we can begin to see the larger picture and see the whole rather than the fragments.

We must achieve distance in order to appreciate the whole. Astronauts have seen the earth from afar and see it in a very different manner than when walking on the earth. An interesting point comes from the study of perception. One question that bothered early researchers was how we were able to see things at different depths. People began to study how subjects were affected by altering the environment. If you ask the subject to close one eye, much of what we see as depth with both eyes is lost. However, if we move our head back-and-forth with one eye closed, our sense of depth is restored. In one incident a military pilot in WW I was trying to land after having lost vision in one eye. Observers on the ground assumed he would crash, although he made a perfect landing. Because he was in motion he could see adequate depth to judge the distance from the runway and land correctly. Other experimenters restricted vision by placing a subject in a room lacking any cues as a gradient such as seen with wall paper, pictures, or hardwood flooring. A standard observation is that looking down a long railroad one can see the rail ties come closer together and the rails appear to converge. This is called a gradient effect and is very important in our perception of depth. After much debate the question was answered with a clever study with infants as young as three months of age. Imagine a glass surface divided into halves with a pattern of four-inch squares on one side and two-inch squares on the other side. Looking from above, an adult would say that the side with the smaller squares was lower than the other side. When an infant was placed on the glass surface at the dividing line of the two sides, the infant would rapidly move to the one with the large squares. The conclusion from this study was that infants as young as three months of age perceive depth. The ultimate conclusion was that the perception of depth is inherent in the human visual system. One can weaken this sense by removing some of the cues used to augment depth, but seeing depth is instinctive and inborn.

We might apply that to life. We are actually born with an inherent sense of the whole but with experience we can alter that tendency to separate the whole into parts and jump from item to item. Imagine someone in an art gallery looking at a painting. What do they see? Unless instructed otherwise, they will see the picture as a whole rather than a painting composed of many dabs of paint. Studies of eye positions and movements while looking at a painting show that our eyes move around and tend to hesitate at significant parts of the painting, but we are seeking the painting as a whole.

Gestalt psychology arose around 1930 in Germany fostered by a group of psychologists who maintained that much of what we perceived was inherent in our body. For example, they cited the perception of figures, the person is clearly distinguished from the background and that figures appear to be large and close to the observer. The German word Gestalt is used to describe the whole of an object. They argued that we perceive the object initially and only later may disassemble it into elements. These psychologists argued that we are born with the ability to see things as whole, or a Gestalt, rather than elements that are brought together by our mental processes. When we look at a person, we see the person as a person, not a nose, right arm, left leg, hair, eyes, etc. We may focus on one aspect such as the eyes, but we still are encountering the person as a whole person. Many American psychologists rejected this theory for several reasons, but, Gestalt Psychology is still alive and well. One can readily relate this work to how the Buddhists teach us to focus on wholes rather than parts of our life's experience.

We can restore a sense of calm to our lives as we look at the whole of an experience rather than its elements. A novice piano player may begin by playing one note at a time but with experience the pianist will start playing segments. If the person tries to look at the separate notes, the flow of the playing is lost. A skilled typist does not type a letter, then another, and then another, and so on. They type words or even sentences. We come into this world seeing things as Gestalts. It is only with analysis can we break them down into parts. Ask this question. Once we break them down into parts, can we reassemble them to recover the whole? Probably not.

The spiritual aspect of this principle is that when one begins to see the unity of all life as a whole, one gains a sense of oneness with the world. This feeling will bring peace to the soul. I am part of a plan or pattern that is greater than me. My role within that plan is the meaning of life for me. My goal is to find that plan and bring meaning into my life. As Richard Bach wrote—"Here is a test to find whether your mission on earth is finished. If you're alive, it isn't."

I am still alive!

## THE BUDDHA'S TEACHINGS ABOUT SEEING THE WHOLE

When we are being mindful we are seeking the whole of our experience of life. Jon Kabat-Zinn in *Wherever You Go There You Are* opened his first chapter writing about mindfulness. Mindfulness he wrote is an ancient Buddhist practice, but is relevant in modern times.

> "This relevance has nothing to do with Buddhism per se or with becoming a Buddhist, but it has everything to do with waking up and living in harmony with oneself and with the world. It has to do with examining who we are, with questioning our view of the world and our place in it, and with cultivating some appreciation for the fullness

of each moment we are alive. Most of all, it has to do with
being in touch."

The Master will teach that your ordinary consciousness is limited by
your attraction to many events occurring in your life. Meditation will
aid you in learning to focus on the whole and ignore the interference
of unessential events.

> "Mindfulness provides a simple but powerful route
> for getting ourselves unstuck, back into touch with our
> own wisdom and vitality. It is a way to take charge of
> the direction and quality of our own lives, including our
> relationships within the family, our relationship to work
> and to the larger world and planet, and most fundamentally,
> our relationship with our self as a person."

Kabat-Zinn adds that our habit of ignoring our present moments by
being attracted to irrelevant happenings interfere with our peace of
mind and health. In many aspects the idea of the whole is so pervasive
in the teachings of Eastern thought that it need not be mentioned as a
special element of life. Mindfulness, meditation, looking inward all
are practices which are taught as a means to bring our focus into the
now, the present moment, and with others which is another way of
seeking the whole rather than the fragments of life.

Eckhart Tolle is a prominent writer and spiritual teacher who
wrote *The Power of Now* and a later book *Stillness Speaks* (2003) in
which he wrote about Now.

> "The division of life into past, present and future is
> mind-made and ultimately illusory. Past and future are

thought forms, mental abstractions. The past can only be remembered Now.

What you remember is an event that took place in the Now, and you remember it Now.

The future, when it comes, is in Now. So the only thing that is real, the only thing there ever is *is* the Now." (Page 40.)

The little book *Stillness Speaks* is essentially an introduction to the thinking of Buddhists teachings, and Now is only one part of his teachings. One final summary statement: Now is the only time there is.

**Use it wisely.**

# CHAPTER EIGHTEEN

# ON THE FEAR OF DEATH

## THE ELEVENTH PRINCIPLE OF ATTITUDINAL HEALING

This principle begins with the statement that "Because love is eternal . . . . Now this statement can be challenged in several ways. I would suggest that if we have begun to live in accordance with the very first principle that we are love, then we might see love as being eternal. For those who do not experience themselves as love may disagree with this statement. The second part of the principle states that death need not be viewed as fearful. That is a very broad statement and will be challenged by many individuals. We will want to examine this latter statement carefully.

The entire principle is:

> *"Because love is eternal, death need not be viewed as fearful.* We begin to let go of our fear of death when we truly believe that what is real never changes and that Love is always present."

I would prefer to state this principle: "As the major teaching of *Attitudinal Healing* is that your essence is love, you can trust that love will be everlasting and would continue after one's death."

However, does that belief allow us to not fear death? Actually, the fear we encounter is greater than any single fear, as we fear the unknown, we fear change, we fear that dying will be unpleasant and probably painful. We also have an existential fear about what happens when one dies.

Westerners have a poor history of dealing with death and dying. Therefore it makes sense that a program like attitudinal healing contain the teaching about love and how it can endure long after one dies, and that one can come to accept dying as a natural stage of life rather than one frightening and unknown. I would agree that if we have a circle of companions, whether relatives or not, who all seek to be love, teach love, and receive love, this circle of companions can be a great resource in our last days of life.

Western religions teach that persons who live a good life and who practice their religion will be selected to enter into heaven. Heaven can be presented as a concept or in some cases as a special place where saved people presumably live for eternity. Not all Westerners believe this teaching, but it is the common way to offer an end to the difficult life that many persons experience. Heaven and eternal life is the reward held out by the church for a God fearing life. By envisioning a different reality, one that considers the end of life as just one more transition in their busy lives, one will have time to fully live life here and now. Those who know you will not stop loving you when you pass, and if you focus on the present and are mindful of the immediate world, you will not dwell on the last transition.

# THE BUDDHA'S TEACHING
# ABOUT TRANSITIONS

Eastern religions have a long history of dealing with life's transitions and death is offered as another transition like being born, reaching adulthood, marrying and having children, becoming enlightened, and finally aging and dying. These religions teach that life is continuous and that upon the transition from this life your soul will continue in another life form. For example, Buddhism teaches that there is suffering in life and you can learn to live with it, work to overcome it, and live in spite of it. That is the essence of the Four Noble Truths which were first taught by Buddha. To quote from the well-known book *The Tibetan Book of Living And Dying,* the Dalai Lama wrote in 1992 that:

> "Death is a natural part of life, which we will all surely have to face sooner or later. To my mind, there are two ways we can deal with it while we are alive. We can either choose to ignore it or we can confront the prospect of our own death and, by thinking clearly about it, try to minimize the suffering that it can bring. However, in neither of these ways can we actually overcome it." (Foreword in the revised edition, 1994.)

I believe the most significant difference in Eastern and Western thinking about life and death is the attitude taken about treatment of illness and disease. In the Western model we orient toward using medicine to prolong life. Thus we are much immersed in a constant barrage of advertisements for hospitals, drugs, health care, and treatments. In the Eastern tradition it is more willingly accepted that death is a part of life and it is to be faced as we face any other major transition in life.

From the book cited above, we find the following quote:

> "When I first came to the West, I was shocked by
> the contrast between the attitudes to death that I had
> been brought up with and those I now found. For all its
> technological achievements, modern Western society has
> no real understanding of death or what happens in death or
> after death." (Tibetan Book of Living and Dying, Page 7.)

Writing further, he commented that most Westerners live with denial
of death or in holy terror of death. Most people live in a spiritual
desert where they imagine this life is all that there is. In conclusion,
the Western attitude about pollution, environmental destruction, and
borrowing against the future, are the result of the belief that there is
no future.

An interesting question I asked years ago of a Biology TA only to
make him angry, that when a cell divides: does the old one die? Does
one continue and one arrives anew? If the two cells are called daughter
cells, what happened to the mother? I believe this puzzle would not
bother a Buddhist as he believes that life continues. Karl Jung offered
the idea of a collective unconscious which was the repository of the
life of our culture that is carried beyond one generation. If we are to
believe that all of life is interconnected, and then we must believe in
the continuity of life, even though my specific self will change into
some unknown form.

From Chapter 9, "All spiritual teachers of humanity have told
us . . . that the purpose of life on earth is to achieve union with our
fundamental, enlightened nature." Recall what Richard Bach wrote:
If you are still alive on this earth, your task on earth has not yet been
done. Live on!

# CHAPTER NINETEEN

# ASKING FOR HELP

## THE TWELFTH PRINCIPLE OF ATTITUDINAL HEALING

Imagine that you are driving on the interstate and you change lanes rather quickly and the other driver gives you a nasty sign. You may have several options.

- Reach for your handgun in the glove compartment and point it at the driver.
- Shake your fist or give in return a nasty sign.
- Smile and wave.

Principle Twelve suggests that you do number three, smile and wave. Let's see why.

The full principle states:

> "We can always see ourselves and others as either extending love of giving a call for help.

Rather than seeing anger and attack, it is always possible for us to recognize a call for help and to answer with love."

From *The Course* we learn that the ego is a major force in one's life but must be overcome to achieve inner harmony. The ego's style is to attack, judge, and criticize. To put to use the lessons of *The Course* we need to be mindful and when someone does something to us, it is often a call for help. If you are in a traffic jam and someone forces their way in front of you, to attack is to allow the ego to dominate your thinking. The ego is that force which makes you believe that you should hurry and get there first, beat out the other person, and win at all costs. Think of all the energy you expend in doing what the ego wants. Think of how fear can motivate us to become sick and depressed. Ask ourselves why we are ill, and we may find that we have been attacking others.

Therefore, the teachings of *The Course* and *Attitudinal Healing* are that you will be able to make peace within yourself by taking option three of the scenario above. By the same reasoning it is better to forgive and release that energy than to hold a grudge. When the ego is dominate, we are constantly alert for any real or imagined hurt, which can drain us of energy and weaken our physical and spiritual efforts to attain peace.

A story about a young girl who jumped off the Bay Bridge to Maryland's Eastern Shore makes this point clearly. She was a good high school student and seemed well. She was a good swimmer and diver but she dwelled on ending her life by jumping from the Bay Bridge. This is a very high bridge, and she did jump. As she was a swimmer her body automatically assumed a proper diving position and she survived the leap. After she was rescued and in the hospital she came upon a magazine article about depression and suicide. She realized that she had been depressed and later she and her mother offered seminars about teenage depression. This girl was making a great call for help which she received as if from a higher source.

The kidnapper who abducts a child to be held hostage is giving a call for help and to use force may not be the best answer for this situation. It is very hard for persons raised in Western culture to understand this principle as it runs counter to the usual capitalistic thinking of competition and getting ahead of your neighbors. Try something like this—the next time you are in line at the local store say hello to the person behind you and offer to let them move ahead. You will find a change in the atmosphere surrounding you and your new friend.

Thomas Moore is a psychotherapist well known for his many books such as *Soul Mates* and *Care of the Soul.* He wrote about a client who came to therapy sessions reeking of garlic. For several sessions Moore did not mention the odor but finally it was too much. When Thomas queried the patient, he answered to the effect that he took garlic pills as a means of testing friendships. If people really liked him, they would overlook the smell. Here is a case where the person is making a call for help through the garlic smell. If he truly wanted friends, he would stop calling for help with garlic and offer his love instead. Moore suggested that he might stop the garlic and find more friends.

Andrew Weil is a physician who has often written about his patients and himself. In his book *Spontaneous Healing* he wrote about his amazing find of a Dr. Wilford who was an Osteopathic Physician of the old school. He was well known for treating children with various ills. He had developed a gadget that vibrated and when he placed it on spots of the body, it worked to release tense muscles and nerves. There are two messages in this story. Weil had taken long trips throughout the world seeking the perfect shaman only to find him next door. Weil's various travels were his call for help which later turned into offering his love to Fulford. He wrote:

> "Discovering Dr. Fulford in my own backyard after chasing all over the world was a powerful lesson: I do not have to look Out There for what I wanted. Neither do most people have to look Out There for healing. Of course, it is worth searching for the best treatment, since treatment comes from the outside. But healing comes from within, its source is our very nature as living organisms."
> (*Spontaneous Healing*, P. 39.)

Another well-known physician is M. Scott Peck famous for his book *The Road Less Traveled*. This book has been a best seller for years and has offered many stories about people searching for something which is within themselves rather than outside. One patient was Ted who had moved into a rustic cabin deep in the woods where he wasted away his time trying to make decisions. One issue was that he had inherited money and did not have to earn any, but he was miserable. He came to Peck for help with his procrastination. His therapy was long and extensive. He related a story about a hurricane in Florida during which he walked out on a pier at the height of the storm. The waves where high and there was a lot of mist around him. He was washed off the pier only to be washed back upon it. He told this story to Peck with little emotion although this was a very powerful call for help. Through his therapy Peck offered Ted love and over time Ted resolved his issues and was ready to move on.

In my recent book *The Fall and Beyond* I wrote about Jane Pauley who was a popular television personality for many years. Yet she had to struggle with life as the life she offered her TV viewers was a false life in that how she lived away from the studio was totally different from how she was seen on television. One of her calls for help came in the form of hives. She suffered a serious case of hives while in elementary school and later about the time she left network television. While seeking help for periods of depression she was diagnosed as a bi-polar or manic-depressive personality. She wrote: "I hadn't been bipolar all along. I had no symptoms that would have alerted the half dozen doctors involved in prescribing medications to me. I was just a lady with hives."

The first set of hives resulted from an incident in the school room when her mother was visiting the class. Thirty years later the hives reappeared and she finally realized that the second appearance of hives was associated with her father's alcoholism, his treatment for alcoholism, and his death.

In her book *A Return to Love* Marianne Williamson wrote about her experiences with *A Course in Miracles.* She was the daughter of a middle-class Jewish family and did attend services with her grandfather many times. Later she gave up on religion and simply wandered around like the orphan she was as depicted by Carol Pearson in *The Hero Within.* She summed up this phase of her life with the following quote: "By the mid-twenties, I was a total mess." She had finally realized she had been calling for help all this time. Next she chanced upon a copy of *A Course in Miracles.* From her experience with *The Course* she began her return to love. *The Course* was a breakthrough experience for her and later she began sharing the teachings of love in *The Course* with a small group of women which began to expand and started her on the journey of returning to love.

Susan Trout in *To See Differently* wrote that this principle encompasses the first eleven principles as it requires integration of those principles into action. When we encounter another person and extend love rather than attack, we will defuse a situation which could become dangerous to us both. We are not trying to change anyone's behavior, but we are changing how we view that behavior. What we are doing is changing how we interpret the behavior of others. Looking back at the experience of Jampolsky when he visited Peru and found the Shaman who treated odd behavior with love, and even more love. This Shaman interpreted the actions of others as a call for help. This is a lesson we all can learn from.

# Go with love.

## Go with love.

### Go with love.

# THE BUDDHA'S TEACHINGS
# ABOUT PRINCIPLE TWELVE

The teachings of the eastern philosophies and religions have this principle embedded in their practices. If you were to ask Lamas to explain aberrant behavior, they would be at a loss as they will see the behavior in a very different light. Their first thought would to be mindful, forgiving, and offering love to that person.

School children who are labeled as hyperactive are seeking attention and giving a call for help. If a teacher or parent can offer the advice that attention span is short, but you can redirect your attention every time it drifts. In my work we found that you can ask the child to sit up straight and look really hard at the material, he or she will gain more. Also, it is useful to let them learn that attention shifts quickly and that they can redirect attention back to the task. With practice and love this child will learn to redirect his or her attention. This is a better practice them offering a stimulant drug, although medication is offered as an easy answer to a complex problem.

When the Buddha began to meditate and gain insight, he was unsure that others would want his teachings. Then he realized that he only needed to offer his teachings allowing others to make the decision about what to adopt and what to ignore. That is a fundamental teaching of all Eastern religion. The writings of the masters are not taught as literal truth, and disciples are encouraged to pick and choose those teachings that are most compatible with their personal belief system. The Master does not tell the novice how to find the way and the novice must find that way on his own. However, the Master does teach to seek the middle way, straying not to the far left or the far right. There are clear parallel between the Buddha and Jesus in how they taught and how that tried to offer wisdom to their followers. If we examine the Christian bible; we find a major difference in how God is pictured in the Hebrew Bible and in the later addition of the teachings of Jesus. The Eastern traditions do not have a hierarchical structure with the Dalai Lama giving the law. The Dalia Lama teaches by parable and storytelling. How one practices whatever form of religion they do is their choice. The enlightened Buddhist will offer love whenever approached. He need not ask whether the person is calling for help as that is the first assumption. But, you answer the call for help with love—always with love.

A major issue in Western life is that we are taught to be independent and therefore, not to ask for help. There is nothing in the teachings of religion that commands us not to ask for help. Yet when young people take an overdose of medication or slice their wrists, they are often making a call for help. That young woman who jumped from the bridge came to understand her feelings of depression and helplessness and traveled with her mother to speak to high school classes about her experience. She was offering these students love.

Perhaps the tale about the wife and the tiger will demonstrate how an enlightened one offers love when one asks for help. The wife of a soldier came to the master after her husband returned from war with an illness that no doctor could cure. The wife tried many things to help her husband but he would not eat, or speak to his wife, or even let her touch him. Distraught she sought the advice of a man who had a reputation of doing great works of healing. When she approached the healer with her tale, he told her there was only one thing he could recommend was that she obtain a whisker from the jowl of a tiger. The woman was greatly disappointed and left but she kept thinking about what the healer had told her. She began to ask friends and neighbors if they knew where she might obtain a whisker from a tiger's jowl and none had a suggestion. She did hear that a wild tiger lived in a cave in a nearby forest and she went there carrying some meat with which to entice the tiger. At first she put the meat well away from the tiger but close enough that he could smell it. The tiger did find the meat and ate it. Day after day she continued to bring meat to the tiger putting it closer and closer to the tiger until she was very near the tiger as he ate. The tiger always took a nap after consuming the food and finally the woman was so close to the tiger when he ate that she was able to remove a whisker from its jowl while he slept. She was overjoyed and ran to the healer with the whisker. She proudly showed the whisker to the healer who took it and threw it in the fire. "What have you done?" she cried. He replied that "My dear woman, a wife who has tamed a tiger has no need for magic medicine to tame her husband." Apocryphal no doubt, but it contains the essence of one asking for help and receiving love.

When Thich Nhat Hanh wrote about the Buddha in *The Heart of Buddha's Teaching,* he wrote that the Buddha repeatedly taught the following:

"I teach only suffering and the transformation of suffering." When you are suffering, by meditation and mindfulness, you will see two reasons for your suffering and work to transform them into peace, love, and joy. "For me this means that suffering is your call for help and you can turn your call for help toward seeking inner peace and love."

Steve Hagen (*Buddhism plain and simple*) told the old story about men sitting at a dinner table with bowls of mouth-watering food but they are not eating as they do not realize that the sharp pains in their stomachs signify hunger. He opined: "This is our basic human situation. Most of us sense that something is amiss with our lives. But we haven't any idea what our problem really is, or what we should do about it." As the master would say, you have the information to cure your husband but you do not know that. By taming the tiger to obtain the whisker you have proved that you have all you need to tame your husband.

I will end this section with a brief Zen poem presented in Hagen's book on page 63.

*Seeker: "Teach me the way to liberation."*
*Zen Master: "Who binds you?"*
*Seeker: "No one binds me."*
*Zen Master: "Then why seek liberation?"*

# PART IV

## TOWARD A NEW WORLD ORDER

We have read enough about the negative factors present in the world today that it is time to move beyond those. We have seen many changes in the world's order with the collapse of the Soviet Union and the globalization of the world economy. There are positive outcomes from these events as well as negative ones. Foremost for our nation is the rise of military power in Asia and the failed attempts by the conservative members of the U. S. government to use our forces to control areas in the world rather than to work for understanding, dialogue, and peace. That is why there is a call for fusion in which America willingly accepts its role as one among all nations rather than one above all nations. We simply cannot rule the world as it is today. In this section I will cite several well-known writers and thinkers with their ideas about how to direct our future toward a humane and peaceful America.

We will begin with the discussion of how America has allowed itself to become immersed in a debate/argument culture. In any debate there are only two sides to any issue and things are presented as if our world is only black and white. A well-known linguist, Deborah Tannen, offers the suggestion that we use dialogue as our basis for discussion rather than debate. In general the writers cited will ask us to listen, not critique or attack, and to offer constructive examples which can lead to compromise.

Jimmy Carter and Paul Rasor point out that our military is huge, very expensive, and has lost its sight of the mission to defend the United States at home. Instead the military is being used to punish countries that do not hew to the American line, and to assert our power and influence over other nations. We call for a self-examination by our nation of this policy and a re-direction of that policy toward one of dialogue and a search for a peaceful solution to world problems.

Thich Nhat Hanh quoted Professor Hans Kung as saying "Until there is peace between religions, there can be no peace in the world." People kill and are killed because the cling too tightly to their own beliefs. He urges us not to believe that ours is the only truth and learn to practice what the Buddhists call nonattachment and to be open to other views.

# CHAPTER TWENTY

# THE ARGUMENT CULTURE

Deborah Tannen

*"The argument culture urges us to approach the world—and the people in it—in an adversarial frame of mind. It rests on the assumption that opposition is the best way to get anything done: The best way to discuss an idea is to set up a debate; the best way to cover news is to find spokespeople who express the most extreme, polarized views and present them as 'both sides' the best way to settle disputes is litigation that pits one party against the other; the best way to begin an essay is to attack someone, and the best way to show you're really thinking is to criticize. (Pp 3-4)*

Without question we are living in what Deborah Tannen called *The Argument Culture*. She subtitled her book Moving from Debate to Dialogue and that is the theme we will follow here. There was a different time where news was reported rather than created, and that time was a good time. One cannot identify any one specific event that started our change but the loss of the Fairness Doctrine has one pivotal point. It was without question easier to apply the fairness policy before the huge expansion of media in America, but, still if we only had that rule to apply to network news it would be an improvement over what we are fed by the 24-hour news programs. How might we change this aspect of our culture? We must start locally rather than the notion that we can somehow change the nature of persons elected to political office. We must start in the home and with our children. We need to set the tone. A major truism in raising children is that they will pay attention to what you do and not what you say. There is a story about a father who took his two sons to play miniature golf and the father noted the prices showing that children under seven played for free. The father asked for two adult tickets and the sales person joked as he said "You could have gotten both boys in free as I would not notice." The father replied "My sons would know."

Once I read a review of the students taking the examination for a National Merit Scholarship. These students had filled out an information sheet in addition to completing the exam. One significant finding was that the winners of scholarships wrote that they had dinner with their parents most every evening at home. It is at the dinner table at home where much of the social learning by children happens in the home under pleasant conditions such as having a family meal. It is at the dinner table that parents can practice dialogue without even making it into a lecture but by example.

Deborah Tannen noted that debate rather than dialogue can be traced to the ancient Greeks and that tradition has continued in Western culture to this day. The most glaring shortcoming of debate is that a false premise underlies the notion that there are always and only two sides to an issue. In actual practice debates a person can and often does take either position and it is a matter of skill with language rather than knowledge or conviction that will win the debate. For most issues there are more than two sides, yet in the current thinking expressed by the media is that everything is black or white. This is simplistic view that does not hold up in actual practice. A recent issue that is an example of the logic of black or white is the concept of global warming. The data are clear that the earth is hotter today than it was 100 years ago. Yet the politicians drew a line in the sand and the conservatives argued that the notion of warming was a fake plot created by liberals. Finally some of the conservatives have admitted that the data are accurate and that warming has occurred. The real issue rarely discussed is whether human beings can do something to slow or stop the warming? That question has not been answered and probably never will be answered.

Returning to our basic theme, we should use dialogue rather than debate; yet to do so we must start locally. Not only in our homes, but in our social clubs, churches, and informal groups; we should strive to remind everyone to be mindful and not attack others. One can question a person without attacking or making it personal. Hopefully we might even see an opportunity in our educational system to demonstrate by example the value of dialogue as an alternative to debate.

# CHAPTER TWENTY ONE

# LIVING BUDDHA, LIVING CHRIST

Thich Nhat Hanh

*"When we see someone overflowing with love and understanding, someone who is keenly aware of what is going on, we know that they are very close to the Buddha, and to Jesus Christ." (Quoted in the Foreword by David Steindl-Rast.)*

*"Real dialogue makes us more open-minded, tolerant, and understanding. Buddhists and Christians both like to share their wisdom and experience. Sharing in this way is important and should be encouraged. But sharing does not mean wanting others to abandon their own spiritual roots and embrace your faith. That would be cruel." (P. 196.)*

The Vietnamese Buddhist Monk Thich Nhat Hahn has written over twenty-five books. He lived in Vietnam during much of the American war against the Viet Cong. He worked for peace throughout this period during which he came to America where he met several theologians interested in bringing that war to an end. In his 1995 book *Living Buddha, Living Christ*, he shows how many elements of Eastern and Western religious thought are alike. Once while attending a conference with many theologians and professors of religion, an Indian participant said: "We are going to hear about the beauties of several traditions, but that does not mean that we are going to make fruit salad." When Hanh was introduced to speak, he countered by stating "Fruit salad can be delicious"

There is an important analogy to the notion of the melting pot taught in schools of America where in fact we have fruit salad as non-European peoples did not melt into the mainline of American society. By the same logic, Hahn acknowledges that one cannot blend all religions into one pot but must recognize that we will have a mixture of religions much as we would have a fruit salad. Carrying the analogy further, we might believe we could puree the various fruits into a uniform liquid mass, but we would lose the unique elements of the individual fruit.

An element of Eastern religion which I find useful is that the teachings of the enlightened masters are offered as examples or guidelines rather than laws or commandments. The master teaches by example and asks that the novice practice the many teachings of the masters. It is through practice that people begin to master the lessons of the masters. This is in contrast to the Jewish-Christian teaching in which there are laws that must be followed and commandments which are offered as teachings coming directly from God. If these laws and commandments are not followed, one has sinned and must make penance to avoid hell. To define one's faith by words is not as meaningful as when one expresses faith through actions.

There is a contrast of the teachings in the Hebrew Bible and those of Jesus as he taught as did the Buddha by stories, parables, practice, and example. In *Living Buddha, Living Christ* Hahn separates the historical Buddha and Christ from the modern understandings of the teachings of Buddha and Christ.

When Jesus taught as written in the Gospel of Thomas:

"If those who lead you say to you, 'Look, the Kingdom is in the sky,' then the birds will get there first. If they say, 'It is in the sea,' then the fish will get there first. Rather, the Kingdom is inside of you, and it is outside of you. When you come to know yourselves, then you will become known, and you will realize that *it is you who are the children of the living Father.* But if you will not know yourselves, then you dwell in poverty, and it is you who are the poverty." (Page xxiii.)

Hahn demonstrated how dialogue is the key to peace. Harken back to Tannen's comments about dialogue. Hahn also noted that sometimes it is harder to have a dialogue with people of your faith than with people of another faith. "But, by understanding your tradition better, you will come to understand the traditions of others." In dialogue both sides must be willing to listen, not criticize, and be willing to change. Real dialogue will bring about tolerance for others and their beliefs

# CHAPTER TWENTY TWO

# THE UNIVERSE IN A SINGLE ATOM

## THE CONVERGENCE OF SCIENCE
## AND SPIRITALITY

### The Fourteenth Dalai Lama

*"Perhaps the most important point is to ensure that science never becomes divorced from the basic human feeling of empathy with our fellow beings. Just as one's fingers can function only in relation to the palm, so scientists must remain aware of their connection to society at large.*

*Science is vitally important, but it is only one finger of the hand of humanity . . ."*

Tenzin Gyatso is the Fourteenth Dalai Lama and fled from Tibet to Northern India in 1959 when the Chinese invaded and occupied Tibet. For the Dalai Lama his move was a significant shift in his understanding of the world from the Tibetan culture. The Tibetan branch of Buddhism is only one of several branches and the formulation of the concept of the Major Lama or Dalai Lama of Tibet occurred in the late sixteenth century CE. He considers himself to be living in exile in Northern India although China has been unwilling to acknowledge him or to leave Tibet.

His Holiness travelled to Europe many times when his home was still in Tibet. He encountered a number of scientists and philosophers of science including Karl Popper. He noted that science was not the slow, gradual accumulation of knowledge as he thought, but that science experienced shifts in the paradigm as the radical change in thinking after the introduction of quantum mechanics. He sees similarity in how Physics is struggling with this new way of thinking to how the Buddhists constantly struggle in trying to understand the world. He found the notion of Popper about falsifiability intriguing as it is similar to a Buddhist's "principle of the scope of negation." He wrote that there is a distinction between what has not been found to what has been found not to exist.

The Dalai Lama stated that his aim in writing the book was not to unite science and spirituality but to study both science and spirituality in a way to develop a "more holistic and integrated way of understanding the world around us." I share this goal, as I too want us to work toward a mutual understanding of the Western world which is heavily invested in the scientific method of empiricism and the Eastern world which just as heavily invested in the spiritual pathway to enlightenment.

Using the example from quantum mechanics about how light can appear as wave form or particular form and that by observing an object, one changes the position or the nature of that object. From Buddhist thinking he cited the notion of emptiness. In Buddhist teaching how we think the world appears is not the way the world actually is. "All things and events, whether material, mental, or even abstract concepts like time, are devoid of objective, independent existence. In a simple statement, everything is a part of the larger whole and when taken out of the context of that whole will appear differently than when within the whole."

There are numerous examples included in this book showing the relationship of knowledge acquired through observation and that obtained through contemplation. Knowledge is not only achieved through deductive reasoning but through its counterpart, inductive reasoning. Following Popper's falsifiability argument the outcome of induction must meet the principle of falsifiability. For the Dalai Lama his exile was like a paradigm shift and he came to understand that the problem with Tibet was its lack of openness to outside knowledge. He has made vast inroads into the heart of Tibetan Buddhist thinking through his many visits with scientists and the knowledge about how science works and when it does not.

For many years the Western world looked down upon the Eastern world though its exploitation of the Orient and the colonization of many areas in the East as with France's occupation of Indochina for many years. Now that the bamboo curtain has been opened, a proper exchange and dialogue between East and West can move forward. With mutual economic advantages of cooperation and understanding, we can avoid a future world war which we all should want to do.

# CHAPTER TWENTY THREE

# DEMOCRACY AND EMPIRE

Paul Rasor, PhD

*"The tension between democracy and empire seems to be a permanent feature of the American condition.*

*By the same token, religious liberals seem cursed to live with the tension between energizing hope and the temptation toward paralyzing cynicism. But cynicism is a luxury of privilege, a negative spirituality that in the end only feeds the forces of empire. We can maintain our hope, and be true to our own religion ideals, if we remember that this very dissonance, this tension that so often frustrates us, can be creative as well as destructive. It can fuel the passion to question, the courage to be prophetic, and the faith to hope. (UU World article, P 35.)*

D r. Paul Rasor is the Director of the Center for the Study of Religious Freedom and professor of interdisciplinary studies at Virginia Wesleyan College. The article cited in this section is adapted from his recent book *Reclaiming Prophetic Witness: Liberal Religion in the Public Square.* His basic theme in his book is stated as follows: "The American impulse toward empire is rooted in the ideologies of militarism and capitalism that, like all ideologies, are grounded in a specific world-view and reflect a set of core values."

(P.32). He sees these values as dogmas and argues that we can understand them if we think of them as theologies rather than as ideologies.

Rasor noted that the theology of violence is not new in American thinking as we can readily see in our image of the west with gun totting cowboys, the use of the Calvary to subdue the natives, our war with Spain and later with Mexico, etc. The current debate over gun ownership and usage is a continuing issue for all Americans. Rasor commented that "Maintaining a global military force of more than 700 bases in over 100 countries is not cheap. The United States spends more today on the military than at any time in its history. By some calculations we spend more on defense than all other nations in the world combined. The upshot is that we have the strongest military machine the world has ever seen. No other nation or bloc of nations even comes close. But our military might has become divorced from its nominal purpose: national defense. No one seriously argues that we need this much military power for actual defense against credible threats. Nevertheless, we take for granted a perpetual state of war and preparedness for war." (P. 33)

Rasor sets the stage for balancing the collective forces toward militarism and empire with our closely held belief that democratic principles will always win out. Rasor cited the philosopher Cornel West. West cited the basic democratic principles which can be traced to the teaching of Socrates as described by Plato. These principles are devotion to questioning and the strong commitment we have for justice.

Rasor made the point the within the impulse toward empire there are certain characteristics that interfere with democracy as the leaders of our country wants citizens who rarely vote and are apathetic about world affairs. These leaders assume that all citizens are patriotic and will readily follow these leaders without comment. They like to think of the citizens as their subjects rather than citizens who are organized and active in political affairs. To achieve these conditions the leaders promote collective fear and indicate the people are powerless to change events. The way the administration acted after the 9/11 attacks on the World Trade Center clearly demonstrate how to accomplish these goals.

The media generally supports the goals of the administration by only offering shallow discussions of significant issues and reports on irrelevant issues in excessive detail to the point that few persons pay any attention to the reports. The practice of polling and reporting these results also fit the desire to control the citizenry as most polls do not meet the standards set by professional polling organizations in that they do not sample randomly and do not include all people in the group from which they sample. Furthermore, polls usually offer only limited answers such as: I agree, I do not agree, or I do not have an opinion; or, Yes, No, Do Not Know. People answering these polls have very different concerns and motivations, yet polling practices lump all these into one category. For example, 47 percent approve of the job the president is doing. This does not explain where the president is failing to meet the needs of citizens.

Rasor has not given up on democracy as he cited the American impulse toward democracy as a long standing presence and is the counter to the impulse toward empire. As Rasor comes from a liberal religious background, it is not surprising that he urges us to become organized and be willing to address issues in the public forum. A fundamental tenet of both Western and Eastern religions is that all persons are equal under god or a higher power. Hence we begin with the idea that all people deserve to be treated with dignity and respect, until persons have shown by their actions they do not deserve dignity and respect.

Rasor traced the origin of our democratic practices to the Greeks and Plato who championed what we call the Socratic method of teaching. This method is evident in the teaching methods of Jesus and the Buddha. Three major characteristics of this method are:

1.  Question your assumptions.
2.  Strive for justice.
3.  Retain a sense of hope.

In a sentence, Rasor believes that America is ready for and needs a revitalization of democracy as a counter to the minority of Americans who strive for empire. And you must remember that this process starts with you and at the local level. Then, and only then, can it work upward.

# CHAPTER TWENTY FOUR

# OUR ENDANGERED VALUES

## AMERICA'S MORAL CRISIS

### Jimmy Carter

*"Our people have been justifiably proud to see America's power and influence used to preserve peace for ourselves and others, promote economic and social justice, raise high the banner of human rights, protect the quality of our environment, alleviate human suffering, and cooperate with other people to reach these common goals. We have learned the value of providing our citizens with accurate information and treating dissenting voices with respect. Most of our political leaders have attempted to control deficit spending, preserve the separation of church and state, and protect civil liberties and personal privacy.*

*All of these historic commitments are now being challenged."*

Jimmy Carter is a well-known political activist who has served his nation as a Naval officer, Governor of the state of Georgia, and as President of the United States. He resides in his home state, and when not traveling he is the main force behind the Carter Center which has world-wide impact. Carter was born James Earl Carter, Jr. in 1924 and entered the Naval Academy in 1942. Carter is a very open and religious person who was raised in the Southern Baptist tradition, although he falls toward the liberal side of that group. The following are excerpts from an op-ed piece he wrote in March of 2003.

Just War, or an Unjust War?

"Profound changes have been taking place in American foreign policy, reversing consistent bi-partisan commitments that for more than two centuries have earned our nation's greatness."

"As a Christian and as a president who was severely provoked by international crises, I became thoroughly familiar with the principles of a just war . . ."

- "The preeminent criterion for a just war is that it can only be waged as a last resort, with all non-violent options exhausted.
- "Weapons used in war must discriminate between combatants and non-combatants.
- "Violence used in the war must be proportional to the injury suffered.
- "The attackers must have legitimate authority sanctioned by the society they profess to serve.
- "The peace to be established must be a clear improvement over what exists.

Using the second war in Iraq Carter mentioned the extensive bombing by aircraft and the many civilian casualties that bombing caused. It was obvious that George W. Bush had not used any non-violent options before attacking Iraq, and his attempt to tie it to the 9/11 attack on the World Trade Center was not proved. If we even try to include how America treated prisoners of war, the conditions set up did not lead to a just war.

Because of the protests, we halted the Selective Service program to the point where our military are not serving their country. In spite of the complaints by the neocons about draftees during the Vietnam War, most draftees served and served well. The major protestors of that war were the elite college students who were deferred from the draft, who we afraid that when the dropped out of college or graduated, they would be sent to war. We have lost the concept of a citizen military and the citizens who serve bring a unique sense of patriotism to unit. In closing Carter wrote: "It is good to know that our nation's defenses against a conventional attack are impregnable, and imperative that America remain vigilant against threats from terrorists. But as is the case with a human being, admirable characteristics of a nation are not defined by size and physical prowess. What are some of the attributes of a superpower? Once again, they might very well mirror those of a person. These would include a demonstrable commitment to truth, justice, peace, freedom, humility, human rights, generosity, and upholding of other moral values."

Carter noted that we have an unprecedented opportunity in the coming future to use our strength and influence wisely and with a generous spirit. It is a time to cooperate with other nations in order to bring about a return to morality in America.

# CHAPTER TWENTY FIVE

# THE PRICE OF CIVILIZATION

## REAWAKENING AMERICAN VIRTUE
## AND PROSPERITY

### Jeffery D. Sachs

*"We need to reconceive the idea of a good society in the early twenty-first century and to find a creative path toward it. Most important, we need to be ready to pay the price of civilization through multiple acts of good citizenship: bearing our fair share of taxes, educating ourselves deeply about society's needs, acting as vigilant stewards for future generations, and remembering that compassion is the glue that holds society together."*

S achs wrote: "The future does not belong to the Tea Party but to America's youth, who are the most progressive and diverse part of American society today. The change will start mainly with the so-called Millennial Generation, those between the ages of eighteen and twenty-nine in 2010, who are socially connected, Inter-net-savvy, and searching for a new mode of social involvement and political engagement. Obama was to be their man, but unless he dramatically alters course, he seems more likely to be a transitional figure than a transformative one." (P. 161.)

Sachs stated that we need greater changes than are being offered at this time. As stated earlier, two of the greatest ethicists in human history were Buddha from the East and Aristotle of the West. In his view both of these thinkers suggested we follow the middle path and to be mindful. These great men taught that the key to fulfillment is the path of moderation, but that this path is hard won and must be constantly sought after throughout one's lifetime through diligence, training, and reflection. In the recent movie Lincoln the character spoke in the metaphor of one walking a tight rope across a great waterfall. The walker must constantly work against those suggesting he go right and those suggesting he go left or he will fall into the water. As President Barack Obama strives for the middle path; critics accuse him of waffling. But he is pursuing the middle path.

Regarding American society Sachs believes we have gone beyond asking to have our needs fulfilled to that of wanting more and more, and ever more. This is the mantra of the person feeling lack, the one person who cannot be satisfied when basic needs are met. For example, Sachs quoted a noted marketing expert as follows:

> "Basic survival goods are cheap, whereas narcissistic self-stimulation and social-display products are expensive. Living doesn't cost much, but showing off does." (Sachs, P. 167.)

A long-standing item for social display has been in America the automobile. This has been well demonstrated by the massive numbers of Hummers, mammoth pickup trucks with huge engines, and all the SUVs that can carry a scout troop but rarely do more than carry a driver and one child headed to the soccer field.

Consider our "War Against Drugs." Why do we use a military metaphor like war to describe the problem in America of persons buying and using illegal drugs? The program should be to educate persons about the harm of all drugs such as nicotine and alcohol recognizing this will not end the problem but may reduce the problem. We should place the responsibility directly on the family for educating their children about drugs hoping to reduce the demand. We cannot stop people misusing drugs by attacking the source of such drugs. In many ways Sachs lays out an idealized plan to reform our government. One can agree with his ideas yet fail to implement them. As in any social change, the change will be gradual and hopefully for the better.

# CHAPTER TWENTY SIX

# CLOSING COMMENTS
# FROM THE AUTHOR

*Until there is peace between religions, there can be*
*no peace in the world.* (Hanh, P. 2.)

When we are trying to bring about a new relationship among nations, we must keep in our minds that every journey starts with one small step. If we are seeking to change our nation we will have to start within our homes by setting the example when we teach our children by what we do, not by what we say. As I think on this topic I am called to remember that great song titled "Teach Your Children Well" written by Graham Nash and first recorded by Crosby, Stills, Nash and Young in 1970.

"Teach the children well . . . and remember that they love you." Few will recall that Walter Mondale ran for the White House in 1984 and used that song in his campaign when he spoke about arms control. This is a lesson that should not be forgotten. As Sachs wrote, the future does not belong to the Tea Party or the extreme right, but to our children. In my life I have tried to set an example which my sons have followed quite well.

As we start on our path toward fusion of East and West we should look to some of our past leaders in this quest. Thomas Merton was quoted as writing that when he met Hanh he saw in him a sense of brotherhood greater than he shared with most Americans. Merton wrote: "We are both monks, and we have lived the monastic life about the same number of years. We are both poets, both existentialists. I have far more in common with Nhat Hanh that I have with many Americans." At another occasion Hanh shared the Holy Eucharist with Dan Berrigan who was an outspoken opponent of our military actions in Southeast Asia. We have the contemporary martyr of Martin Luther King, Jr. who carried his message of love and peace until he was brought down by an assassin's bullet in Memphis and the similar work of Nelson Mandela who spent years of his life in the South African jail for his attempt to bring justice to his people. Each of these great men began their journey to peace with one small step and we are wise to walk behind them.

Yet it is not only men who have affected my understanding of the role of religion in world politics. I first became aware of the work of Isak Dinesen when I attended the movie "Out of Africa." I was so moved by that event that I began to get copies of her books. Her formal name was Karen Blixen while she wrote under her pen name. What struck me was that while she professed to be a Unitarian she often would attend the Midnight Mass at a Catholic Church as she liked the music and ritual. Once she invited her African assistant to attend and he was shocked as he had spent time in a Presbyterian Hospital when he was ill and the nurses warned him never to enter a Catholic Church or he would be damned to hell. Isak commented that the various countries from Europe represented in Africa brought with them their personal religion and indoctrinated the people with their specific religious teachings to the exclusion of all others. More recently the noted author Phil Caputo wrote a serious work about the civil war in the Sudan and how the religions missionaries tried to force the Christian view on the people while we're trying to get food to the starving people in the south. As it became apparent, the attempt to bring the Christian religion to the natives worked at cross purposes with the attempts to bring aid amidst the dreadful political situation. One can go on about problems and issues in America or in the West in general, but that is not wise. I hope to have made my point that all is not well in the Western world as we have lived it in the last sixty or so years. I harken back to the days before America decided that its military might would be used to force peace onto the world. This was the call for empire which has brought us to our state today where we have continuous war without any apparent end. We came out of World War II as the major force in the Western world but have misused that power. One sad issue was our gross, exaggerated fear of communism as shown by our government's misguided actions during the McCarthy era and the long-lasting change in the pledge of allegiance when "under God" was added. I would argue that God should not be capitalized and that the term god is generic and not restricted to what many Americans believe is the exclusive god of the Christians in the U. S.

I offer this work as my personal view of what we can do to build a true world of nations which share the values of openness, dialogue, and peace as described in this last Part of *Fusion*.

# Attribution

The Cover

Source: Own Work By R. Gopakumar http://en.wikipedia.org/wiki/
File: The_Birth_of_the_son_of God.jpg